Pensive Pauses
Epigrams and Poems

Pensive Pauses
Epigrams and Poems

By
Joseph Mileck

Pensive Oasis
Berkeley, California
2016

ISBN Print: 978-0-9982685-0-7
ISBN ebook: 978-0-9982685-1-4

Printed in the United States of America

Design and Layout: Rick Soldin (book-comp.com)

Pensive Oasis, Berkeley, California

Thought begets Thought

Contents

Foreword

The Greek Epigram

Our Western World's epigram—poetry at its briefest—has had a long and checkered history. It all began in Ancient Greece. At its earliest, the Greek epigram was but a commemorating inscription on a gravestone or monument. In time, simple inscription moved from stone to papyrus, became an elegiac couplet, and then ballooned to a four-to six-line poem. Somber one-line inscriptions became pithy verse: eulogistic, satirical and moralistic comment that often spared neither friend nor foe. Brevity, point and sting became and remained the intrinsic properties of Greece's long and rich trail of epigrams.

Meleager of Gadara was the foremost of ancient Greece's many author-compilers of epigrams. His compilation of the first century B.C.—a collection of epigrams of his and those of many of his predecessor epigrammatists—together with several subsequent compilations, became known in the 10th century as the *Greek Anthology*. This early collection of compilations, further augmented until the outset of the 17th century, was to have considerable influence on the 16th century vernacular literatures of Italy and France, and was even to attract a rush of scholarly interest as late as the 20th century: an English translation of the *Greek Anthology* appeared in 1916, followed by a French in 1928, and the anthology's cultural influence was widely scrutinized (e.g. James Hutten, *The Greek Anthology in Italy*, 1936; *The Greek Anthology of France*, 1946). This modern-day interest in Greece's ancient epigrams has continued to simmer to the very present.

The Latin Epigram

*U*nlike Greece, Ancient Rome was not blessed with a *Latin Anthology* and resultantly, most of the collections of epigrams written by many of its major writers—among them Domitius Marsus, Marcus Lucan, Cornifius and Cosconius—went the way that most things go. The foremost among Rome's authors whose epigrams survived were Gaius Valerius Catullus (84–54 B.C.), Decimus Junius (60–140 A.D.) and Marcus Valerius Martialis, Rome's master of the epigram. Martial was for Ancient Rome what Maleager of Gadora was for Ancient Greece.

The Latin epigram peaked in Martial's mordantly satirical asides. Though obviously much indebted to Greece's pioneering of the genre, his epigrams, and Latin epigrams in general, are unmistakingly Roman. In matter, they tend to be more personal, in manner, more terse, and in wit, more acridly satirical than their Greek counterparts. Martial spared neither the mighty nor the lowly, and neither friend nor foe. All were dispatched with abandon, some unabashedly eulogized and others caustically reduced, and liberal obscenities lent Martial's exposure of his society's faults and foibles a popular common touch.

In time, Martial's more than 1500 extant epigrams became major models for both England's and France's epigrammatists. Indeed, the *Martial epigram* became the *European epigram*. Like Greece's, Rome's epigrams have continued to preoccupy translators and scholars to the present. Two volumes of English translations appeared in 1919 (W.C.A. Ker), three volumes of French translations followed in 1930 (H.J. Isaac), and the Latin epigram tradition has continued to attract scholarly attention (e.g., W.M Lindsay, 1929; C. Giarratano, 1951; R. Helm, 1951).

The European Epigram

*I*n the dark Middle Ages, European literary interest in the epigrammatic tradition of Greece and Rome was negligible. It was not until the Renaissance's re-awakened interest in the literatures of Ancient Greece and Rome that Europe discovered and began to cultivate the epigram vernacularly. Martial's Latin pungent and often indecent epigrams served as major models for France's, England's and Germany's epigrammatists of the 17th and 18th centuries. Clément Marot (1496–1544) and Mellin de Saint Gelais (16th century) pioneered the French epigram, Ben Jonson (1573–1637) and Robert Herrick (1591–1674) ushered in the English epigram, and Friedrich von Logau set the German epigram on its way.

Europe's new literary interest spread rapidly. Many of France's, England's and Germany's poets began to explore the novel possibilities of the new genre. France's most prominent writers/intellectuals—among them, François Malherbe (1555–1625), François de La Rochefoucauld (1613–1680), Nicolas Boileau (1636–1700), Voltaire (1694–1718), Rousseau (1712–1778) and Victor Hugo (1812–1885)—took to the epigram like ducks to the water. Many of England's leading poets—among them, John Dryden (1631–1700), Matthew Prior (1664–1721), Jonathan Swift (1667–1745), Alexander Pope (1688–1744), and Walter Savage (1775–1864)—and even a number of its prominent novelists—among them, George Meredith (1828–1909), Oscar Wilde (1854–1900), G.W. Shaw (1856–1950), and Hilaire Belloc (1870–1953)—became enthusiastic practitioners of the epigram. Germany's preoccupation, trailing that of France and England, peaked in the 18th century (Gotthold Lessing, 1729–1781; Wolfgang Goethe, 1749–1832; and Friedrich Schiller, 1755–1805), gradually declined in the 19th century (Eduard Mörike, 1804–1875, and Friedrich Hebbel, 1813–1863), and has—like France and England's love affair with the epigram—but simmered on to the present.

France, England and Germany's present-day smoldering interest in the epigram may linger on and then eventually simply wither away, or it may again become the vigorous genre it once was, and hopefully sooner than later. What better setting for a likely renaissance of the epigram than the global social chaos of the 21st century. My own rush of some 4500 epigrams (*A Medley of Piquant Poetry and Edgy Epigrams*, 2010; *More Salt and Pepper*, 2012; and *Pensive Pauses*, 2016) may become a part of this envisaged rebirth of the genre.

Definition

*P*rotean as it has been in its intent, matter, manner and tone, the epigram has to date defied fixed precise definition. Given that the epigram is but one of many generally familiar related terse expressions, definition by association, though perhaps less telling, is clearly more ready and inviting than definition by direct characterization.

There are the saying, saw, maxim, axiom, motto, adage, apothegm and aphorism, and all are terse familiar expressions of wit or wisdom or truth, all are humorous, satirical or paradoxical, and all are intent upon alerting, startling or shocking. It is to this family of popular utterances that the epigram belongs, and it is a discerning association with these common sayings that best defines the protean epigram.

A Family

Epigrams, proverbs, aphorisms and saws,
Maxims, adages, sayings and mottoes,
All say much in their brevity,
All words of wit and words of wisdom,
All weighty in their philosophical gaze,
All are informative and all tease thought,
All easily memorized, all readily recalled,
And all should be heeded though all can be challenged.

Pensive Pauses

The 3000 or more epigrams of the present collection and the some 1500 previously published (*A Medley of Piquant Poetry and Edgy Epigrams*, 2010; *More Salt and Pepper. Poems and Epigrams*, 2012) were inspirationally indebted to the European epigram, but only loosely mindful of the intent, matter, manner and tone of their models. In their intent to alert and to invite or compel reciprocal thought, these epigrams, unlike the traditional epigram, are general and mild rather than personal and sharp; in their preoccupation with the human and social condition, their moralizing, psychologizing and philosophizing, and in their focus on religion and human values, they are again more general than personal. With their characteristic end- and internal rhymes, their common alliterations and parallel structures, these predominantly one-line epigrams tend to be more terse and more poetic than the traditional European epigram. In tone they are also less crusty and less blunt.

The poems of *Pensive Pauses*, and those of *A Medley of Piquant Poetry and Edgy Epigrams* (2010) and of *Salt and Pepper* (2012), are one of a kind. Like their companion epigrams, they are by and large reflective, pungent and provocative. In matter, like the epigrams, they focus critically upon the human condition and upon the social, political and cultural worlds, and in manner, they range from traditional stanzas, meter and rhyme to casual free verse. In mood, both poems and epigrams of *Pensive Pauses* continue to be somber, satirical, facetious, and hopeful, and in intent, they continue to alert, clarify, unsettle, amuse and to prod readers to distill their own thoughts and to write their own poems and epigrams.

May the epigrams and poems of *Pensive Pauses* chance on curious minds, and may they stir to advantage!

August 2016

EPIGRAMS

An epigram is a dwarfish whole
with wit and soul.

*R*ights and wrongs are relative absolutes.

Absolute freedom spells absolute anarchy.

Doing nothing is doing something.

Facts are stuff, opinions are fluff.

Don't die before you are dead.

Outrage begets outrage.

Commonalities are building blocks, differences are road blocks.

It is the heard that is heeded and not the said.

Death is life's only certainty.

Have "ought" you are somebody, have "nought" you are nobody.

Provocation invites reciprocation.

Forethought and restraint not afterthought and regret.

Bark but do not bite.

Rights do not rescind wrongs.

To be certain about everything is to know nothing.

It is not the fool alone who is foolish.

Poets distil, novelists inflate.

For death there is no cure.

Human beings are as destructive as they are creative.

Men assert, women nurture.

Opinions are only as good as they are informed.

Virtue is its own reward.

To ignore the past is to deprive the present.

Outer beauty entrances, inner beauty enhances.

A face is a window to a person.

Some do and some don't. Some can't and some won't.

To live is to struggle and then to die.

To think too much is to do too little, and to do too much is to
think too little.

Too much freedom intoxicates, too little freedom asphyxiates.

Some people refresh, most distress.

To indulge too much in the present is to jeopardize the future.

To get what one wants, one must know what to do.

Don't squeeze a lemon to get orange juice.

To press an issue is only to create a bigger issue.

Know before passing judgment.

The future is but more of the past.

To decide where you're going,
Decide where you've been.

To know the cause is half the cure.

Right is might.

History does not judge, it records.

Wars are the epitome of madness.

Forgiveness is the milk of understanding.

Military bravery is characteristically sheer folly.

Emigration is hopelessness and escape,
Immigration is quest and hope.

The froth and dross of life are ready comfort and deadly snare.

Death is freedom, a release abhorred.

Descriptions are not explanations.

Women produce and men destroy.

Aloneness is existential plight,
Loneliness is individual blight.

Wealth is not wisdom and girth is not substance.

Success trumps ethics.

Comfort dampens, greed enervates.

A fight though won, leaves nothing done.

Individuals can be rational, crowds are emotional.

Persistence is a lever for every endeavor.

Women produce and preserve,
Men polish and demolish.

Women look for a mate,
Men look for a date.

To be just is always to be correct,
To be correct is not always to be just.

Empires are born of the sword, live by the sword and die by the
    sword.

Love is chance, death is certainty.

The struggle of life is a meld of joy and grief.

Actions are telling, words resound.

Life is fight and blight and not kiss and bliss.

The alike flock together like birds of a feather.

Change is life's sole constant.

Life is less spirit than it is flesh.

To have more is all too often to be less.

Lies are as common as flies.

Reality obligates and dream liberates.

Tomorrows are shaped by todays.

We are all but the children of children.

Emotions don't lie, but reason is suspect.

The body is what the mind makes of it.

Self-evaluation is self-aggrandization.

To take is natural, to give is cultural.

Fighting reduces both winner and loser.

Cowards die many times, heroes but once.

To stoke or to damp? The choice is yours.

Those that have, should give.

Barkers are many, biters are few.

One person's treasure is another person's trash.

Personality and chance determine the dance.

To be too open-minded is to be empty-headed.

To vacillate is to abdicate.

Where there is carrion there are vultures.

War is choice and not chance.

Many know but few care.

We assume too much and know too little.

Preoccupations reveal the person.

Empty heads have closed minds.

Weather is changeless in its ever changing course.

Day reveals and night conceals.

Empathy is a friendly bridge, antipathy is a hostile ridge.

Prayer comforts, does not cure.

What is good for the wanting many can also be good for the wealthy few.

Discontent is fertile soil for anger and foment.

Instigation rouses, mitigation douses.

To help is laudable, to hamper despicable.

The poor may be rich and the rich may be poor.

Some plants grow best in rocky soil, as do some humans in bitter toil.

The physically weak are often the mentally strong.

Time is marked by the milestones along the highway of change.

Moderation can ameliorate, extremes will agitate.

One person's thinking is food for another's thought.

War is hysteria, peace is euphoria.

Belief and doubt are birds of a feather that flock together.

Earth's our fact and heaven's our fancy.

Nurture the living and let die the spent.

Heaven or hell, the choice is yours, as too the rewards of each.

Wars spawn empires and empires wage wars.

Hope, laughter and sleep the blues at bay do keep.

Heaven is an ardent belief in better possibility.

Goods dwarf goodness.

Women lure men and men pursue women.

Think and do or be done in.

Everybody can do better, even the best.

Read and heed, don't just read.

If not at peace with the self, peace with the other is unlikely.

Self- and other- deception is a well-honed art.

Pain is gain not bane.

Better to accommodate than try to eliminate.

Generosity is lean and greed is mean.

Rest is won when labor's done.

Fashioned truths fashion wars.

Good deeds spread good seeds.

Love elevates, hate denigrates

After work, 'tis best to rest.

Patience tempers endurance.

Laughter lightens and anger tightens.

Afflictions are many and blessings are few.

Admonitions are both censure and hope.

The macro world overwhelms, the micro world astounds.

The wealthy control and the poor are controlled.

Social inequities are iniquities.

To become a writer, one must first be a reader.

Struggle and strife are the stuff of life.

To assist another is to aid a sister or brother.

To teach is to enlighten, to preach is to frighten.

Choice is to have a voice.

Ambition has restless legs.

The venal are the vile.

Iniquities are flagrant ubiquities.

Bridges invite and unite, walls bar and ban.

Justice denied is justice defiled.

Adamant certainty is veiled insecurity.

Each is what each chooses to be.

Awe befits life, awful befits the world of politics.

Revenge begets revenge.

Lie is pervasive while truth is elusive.

Everything has a price and everything is both good and bad.

Think before holding forth.

Look backward when looking forward.

Humor is grace, violence is disgrace.

Flaws can be virtues.

Success and failure are contrary mates.
The former elates, the latter grates,
And neither is known but for the other.

Any religion is both deflation and enervation.

To describe is science, to define is philosophy.

To have everything is to have nothing.

Music is the panacea of panaceas.

Today's pig is tomorrow's pork.

There is no money in virtue.

Greed knows no limits.

Good health is real wealth.

Life has no U turns.

A door that has never been opened, cannot be closed.

To test the impossible is to tease the possible.

Excess knows no excess.

The culpable should be held accountable.

Not to try is not to succeed.

Success exhilarates and failure humiliates.

Better to try and fail than to fail to try.

Patience and a snare will catch many a hare.

Confidence is the road to competence.

The wealthy few and the many poor are co-dependents.

Truths are believed, facts are known.

Better neither than either miser or spendthrift.

Some dream, more scheme and most just scream.

All goes as the water flows and the wind blows.

Memory preserves what time destroys.

Life is rife with strife.

Contentment is a coat of many colors.

What one is is less important than what one does with what one is.

Resentment knows no contentment.

Anger has never been one of life's endangered phenomena.

Empathy binds, antipathy grinds.

Intelligence is common, wisdom is rare.

Freedom is not a carte blanche.

In the kingdom of capitalism, morality is an anachronism.

Unbridled freedom is fare for gods alone.

Most work to live, some live to work.

Veracity is a quality well-known for its scarcity.

Less can be more and more can be less.

Happiness is a state of mind and not the state of one's purse.

Choice is telltale.

Differences make the person.

Here but briefly and gone forever.

The milk of human kindness is very nourishing.

The strong and the wealthy are arrogant and healthy,
The poor and the weak are sickly and meek.

Joys are ever few and sorrows are never new.

Every living is ever becomes a was.

Some people are good for no good reason.

An itch untended is a scratch offended.

An itch deserves a scratch.

Difference makes a difference.

Not to know oneself is not to know others.

Appreciate, don't deprecate the different others.

To do well is to feel well.

Not knowing is not a virtue.

Life is struggle and strife.

More than one, spells dispute.

Criticism invites antagonism.

To lose is not always loss.

Nothing is possible or impossible until it is tried.

Every change is a challenge.

Some awaken when they fall asleep.

Challenge is stimulating and intimidating.

Every truth bears scrutiny.

Violence is a reflex response to difference.

Some assert themselves in discussion, others in quarrel.

——

One can learn as long as one can squirm.

No one washes a rented car.

To self-correct is to self-protect.

To know nothing is to do nothing.

All thought means no action, and all action means no thought.

Too little choice annoys, too much choice cloys.

A brain not used is a brain abused.

Kind words and helping hand praise and respect command.

Wealth is a burden, poverty is a curse.

Too much is burden, too little is blight.

Kindness is reflective action, violence is reflexive reaction.

Generosity leaves one with both less and more.

Love is no less blind than hate,
The former aggrandizes, the latter minimizes.

Human beings are ends in themselves and not just means to ends.

Need is must, want is lust.

Good health is true wealth.

Expectations are direction and motivation,
They are also exasperation more often than exhilarations.

To teach is to enlighten, to preach is to frighten.

Much is not what it seems to be.

Kindness is empathy, sympathy and humanity.

Patriotism, right or wrong, is chauvinism, pure and simple.

Some are given to good will, more are taken with ill will.

To care is to share.

Engineers build, designers sell.

Problems tease, resolutions please.

To settle for less is to end with more.

Too much choice means no choice.

War anywhere is a threat to peace everywhere.

A love that possesses is a love that distresses.

Erotic love is short-sighted and intoxicating, platonic love is clear-sighted and exhilarating.

Life's not meant to be a seamless revelry.

A country is defined by its culture.

We know we think and we think we know.

The physically awkward are often the mentally agile.

The healthy are the wealthy.

Wisdom is not a commodity.

Fools are ubiquitous, the wise are inconspicuous.

Struggle and strife are the stuff of life.

To understand is not necessarily to forgive.

To become more informed, more reflective and more humane is to become more human.

Good luck inflates, bad luck deflates.

Victory and defeat walk hand in hand.

What is distillate for one is dross for another.

Absolute freedom spells absolute chaos.

Head and heart wend their separate ways.

Today's boon may be tomorrow's drag.

Unqualified freedom is more deadly potion than healing lotion.

Women are tame, men have to be tamed.

Too many are too little of *more* and too much of *less.*

Virtues are extolled and vices are practised.

The present is aftermath and harbinger.

Time is timeless.

Science explains, it does not prove.

Religion does not prove, it states.

War for peace is less justification than obfuscation.

Most know little and are mindful of less.

Truths are compasses, opinions are weather vanes.

There is no second chance to make a first impression.

Good-will invites good-will and malice breeds malice.

Better a healthy mind and a healthy body than a healthy purse.

Improvement demands decision and movement.

Imitation is stagnation, innovation is transformation.

A duck waddles and quacks, it does not strut and crow.

Opposites are two of a kind.

Life and sex are co-dependents.

We do to learn and we learn to do.

Success inflates and failure deflates.

Giving is twice rewarding.

Wars do not rectify, they only lay waste and horrify.

Life is a bitter-sweet pill, not a piece of cake.

Truths are terse and lies are wordy.

Normalities are fluid, not fixed.

Shame knows right and wrong.

Money has wings.

When in doubt, rout about.

Perspicacity and sagacity walk hand in hand.

Commitments are admirable, excuses are abominable.

Let live what wills to live.

Captain your own ship, chart your own journey and live your own fate.

Self-realization is life-fulfillment.

Taste baits, a meal sates.

Egoism is natural, altruism is cultural.

Everyone uses everyone.

The jungle is fit for the fit.

Life has always been an exacting jungle.

Pain and gain are companion travellers.

To help those in need is a worthy deed.

Good deeds are good seeds.

Excuses are evasions, commitments are engagements.

Change for change's sake is an exciting affliction.

Everything comes and goes and nothing is here to stay.

All happenings have both positive and negative consequences.

Needs are necessity, wants are luxury.

The old is not categorically bad and the new is not categorically good.

We know we think and we think we know.

There's no gain but that there's also loss and there's no loss but that there's also gain.

Every day is what was, is, and will be.

Discussion tends to stimulate, argument tends to alienate.

Enjoy agreement and appreciate disagreement.

Dreams realized are dreams spent.

We arrive in pain, lead stressful lives, and depart in pain.

Years alone wise do not make.

Humanism edifies, technology reifies.

Too many solutions are but problems in the making.

To serve others is to serve the self.

Hate acerbates and enervates, love placates and generates.

Love is to life what hate is to death.

Possessions too often possess their possessors.

Good will is good diplomacy.

Words and peace trump weapons and war.

Good will is both good soil and good seed.

Silence is very telling.

The *narrow path* is too narrow for too many.

Emotions of a kind tend to attract emotions of that kind.

The known leaves at ease, the unknown puts on guard.

We think we know and know we don't.

Comfort and solace are found in togetherness.

Hardhearted prosper, softhearted flounder.

The young look to the future, the old look to the past.

Love is the glue that binds us, hate is the poison that blinds us.

The short are more quick than fast and the tall are more fast than quick.

Youth is idolized and age is stigmatized.

Doors invite and fences forbid.

Manipulation is an abomination.

A dyed-in-the-wool sceptic is a dour stick-in-the-mud.

Take care of your body and mind and they will take care of you.

Interest in yesterday is a concern about tomorrow.

Total liberty is total insanity.

Unqualified liberty spells unacceptable inequity.

Greed is pathological, need is circumstantial.

Wealth makes not for spiritual health.

Poverty is not a novelty.

Hawk and prey have had their day.

To politic is not to govern.

100% right is moral failure, as is 100% wrong.

We gain when we lose and we lose when we gain.

To choose is to gamble.

Today's villains are tomorrow's heroes.

Feed need and bleed greed.

Oaks beget acorns and acorns beget oaks.

Common sense is not common.

Expediency trumps principle.

Relativists know no absolutes, and absolutists know no compromise.

Practised principles are a luxury.

Certainty should always be called into question.

Flowers attract and weeds distract.

Promise is commitment and commitment is obligation.

Fortune is as fickle as weather.

Cultures are as demanding as they are rewarding.

Disbelievers believe as do believers.

Pragmatism and idealism are as night the day.

To do takes effort and time, to wish takes neither.

Ideologists and idealists are anything but birds of a feather.

Marketers are psychologists without peers.

One kills the other to oneself survive.
This feat, alas, will leave no one alive.

Goodness and greatness are rarely bedfellows.

Life is a circle, not a straight line.

Consistency is largely a fantasy.

Legality plus morality equals civility.

Morality will lead to heaven or hell,
Legality will lead to home or cell.

To be something to everybody is to be nothing to anybody.

Nobody can be somebody for everybody.

To share with others is to care for brothers.

Passions are not quenched, they drown or wither.

Some hunger for money, others for power, and all too many just
hunger for food.

To feel, to think and to do is to be and to become.

To talk too much is to say too little.

Expertise is respected, popular opinion prevails.

To respect is to be respected.

Racial and sexual slurs are not free speech.

To kill is to be killed.

Humor is oft born of gloom and desperation.

The unprivileged are legion.

Reciprocity—yes, retaliation—no!

More poetry and less politics!

Heed and heal, don't just bark and bite.

Some enjoy, more endure.

Lawyers do not practise theology, and priests do not practice law.

When blush leaves bloom, nought's left but gloom.

Bark if you must, but do not bite.

When face thins and hair grays, it's high time to mend your ways.

To nip all expectations is to scotch all disappointments.

Violence is a short cut to nowhere.

My name is Sisyphus, as too is yours.

Today's dreams are tomorrow's realities.

Words don't retell, they remake.

Capitalism targets wealth, socialism targets poverty.

When principle fails, politics prevails.

Defensiveness is questionable responsiveness.

Nothing is here to stay. All will away.

Virtues can become vices.

Poverty breeds crime and crime breeds poverty.

Inspiration without perspiration invites frustration.

To blame is to shame, to praise is to raise.

The many below are needy, the few above are greedy.

Greed dines and need whines.

To avenge is but to invite revenge.

Denigration invites retribution.

The poor sow, the wealthy reap.

The greedy are mean and the needy are lean.

Each is chance and choice. Grieve and rejoice.

To cope, persist and hope.

Moderation is an obligation.

To persist is to persevere.

Reason flails, emotion prevails.

Our commonalities attract and bind, our differences repel and blind.

The strong will fight, the weak seek flight.

Our common humanity is primary, such as race and ethnicity are secondary.

Greed is rarely need.

To be too certain is a curtain.

Where one sits determines where one stands.

Whence, whither, why, in vain for answers cry.

Time is space and space is time.

Action is to activity what progress is to movement.

The passing years bring passing joys and passing tears.

Teaching spells giving and learning spells growing.

Curiosity together with thought makes possibility of the impossible.

We are but what our needs and passions make of us.

All things alive are but manifestations of life, and not life itself.

Ambition makes and breaks.

There is never a plus but that there is a minus.

Life balances its realities.

Enough is rarely enough.

To fail to extend oneself is to fail.

Benevolence purrs and invites, malice growls and bites.

When trust takes wing, chaos takes hold.

Respectability spells acceptability.

To say nothing is to say something.

Youth's becoming is an adventure, age's unbecoming, misadventure.

Traffic lights are not suggestions.

What is, is ever changing.

Uncertainty is one of life's certainties.

Change for change's sake is questionable change.

The young look to the future, the middle-aged are given to the present, and old age dwells on the past.

Mothers hover and smother, fathers bumble and grumble.

Neither morality nor legality is beyond frivolity.

Life is a mix of lot, chance and choice.

Universals are lot, particulars are circumstance.

Choice is gain and choice is pain.

Even a nobody is a somebody.

Stealing replenishes, buying diminishes.

Dogs give their paws in expectation, while cats swat in sharp frustration.

The factual is needed, the perceptual is heeded.

Pine, but do not whine.

But to play, is to waste away.

Ablution is the Hindu's solution.

Not to know, is a woe.

What you know, is not just for show.

Humans fashion culture and cultures refashion humans.

A fixed mind is a blind mind.

Curiosity kills more rats than cats.

When life ails, pain prevails.

Actions have their predictable reactions.

The unknowing and inept become society's abiding kept.

That Christmas comes but once a year is indeed good cause for cheer.

Loquacity is more chatter than matter.

Opacity, mendacity and rapacity are rarely in short supply.

Perspicacity, tenacity and sagacity are ever in short supply.

The poor take what they are given and they are given very little.

Punishment is retribution, prevention is solution.

Quarrel blinds, discussion binds.

Choice is pain no less than joy and gain.

Worm, squirm and learn.

Faults are more obvious than virtues.

Flaws in thinking are thine and mine.

Brawn moves things, the imagination creates things.

Judgment should be informed opinion and not reflex response.

When morality fails, anarchy prevails.

Attractions can be costly distractions.

Modesty and shame are not the same.

Humility humanizes, arrogance antagonizes.

Pearls are to girls what toys are to boys.

Imagination is emancipation.

Patriotism is personal and nationalism is political.

Love embraces, hate erases.

Chance is adventure, choice is security.

Each, though other, is a sister or a brother.

Each is chance, and each, a solo dance.

Life is brief, toil, joy and grief.

Patrimony and matrimony went their separate semantic ways.

To give heed is to succeed.

Of the vast unknown, but little is knowable.

Good health is true wealth.

Not to know is not to grow.

To possess is to be possessed.

The self-relationship is the most important of human relationships.

To come to grips and to terms with the other, one must first come to grips and to terms with the self.

Know thyself is a promising prelude.

The young are would-bes, the old are has-beens.

Insistence invites resistance.

Experience plus reflection enhance self-perception.

Self-knowledge precedes other-knowledge.

Facts inform, truths guide.

Appearance but attracts, substance engages.

Money, like sex, has become pure reflex.

Justice is to prosecution what injustice is to persecution.

Racism and economic disparity have never been a rarity.

God talks to some, science proclaims to others.

Too much talk and too little walk characterizes too many social issues.

For the weak, life has always been bleak.

The meek are silent and the bold are loud.

The humble bow and the arrogant strut.

Anger is both shield and spear.

Manage the avoidable and avoid the unmanageable.

Thought is demanding, feeling is reflexive.

Objectivity is an idea, not a fact.

Concerts are as bountiful as receipts.

The hawks screech and swoop, the doves coo and woo.

Pragmatism is a practice, ideology is a passion.

Intransigence digs in, intelligence moves on.

Challenge stimulates, convenience only accommodates.

Polished marketeers are but high-class racketeers.

Humanity, thy name has become futility.

Inhumanity has become a global calamity.

Life has always been bleak for the humble, the weak and the meek.

Hyperbole is more loquacity than it is mendacity.

Expediency is the morality of pragmatism.

Abstinence is deficit, indulgence is surfeit, and moderation is neither.

Ill will is a perverse thrill.

Good will often prevails when all else fails.

Today is tomorrow's determinant.

The talented different make the difference.

Atheists argue that they know, and agnostics admit that they don't.

Skeptics believe nothing, and nihilists discount everything.

To do one's best is to deserve one's rest.

To read is a must, to write is a thrust.

Each makes his/her own weather.

To pause is to recharge.

Look before you walk and think before you talk.

Silence is both cowardly retreat and wise abstention.

Youth is uncouth and age is sage.

Differences of opinion should stimulate, not agitate.

Thought leads to reflection and contemplation to meditation.

Meditation is to contemplation what reflection is to thought.

Too little is known about too much.

Too little, too late. A common fate.

There are thinkers and feelers, and then there are the sleepers.

Too much, too soon is not a boon.

We are what we were and will be what we are.

There is no return to what once was.

We never become what we never were.

Frivolity, thy home is ubiquity.

Nothing is, all is flux.

Poverty chokes, wealth bloats.

The poor drown in poverty and the rich float in wealth.

Gain without loss is popular dross.

Conscience is needed and should be heeded.

Clothing protects and fashion exploits.

Men take and break, women lure and endure.

Our fair earth is wealth's dear heaven, and the fair beyond of
    myth is poverty's vain hope of heaven.

Moderation should be moral obligation.

Unqualified freedoms invite untoward liberties.

To mull is in due time to cull.

For some, work is play, and for others, play is work.

To assume blame is to assuage guilt.

One can't eat pork but that one kills a pig.

An unhappy wife makes for marital strife.

Finders should be kind and losers should be thankful.

A seed is much in little.

Good teachers are good learners.

Freedom of expression is not freedom of transgression.

To use another is to abuse a brother.

Hindsight is but belated insight.

Money may smell but poverty stinks.

To deceive another is to deceive a sister or a brother.

Where there is life, there is strife.

Huff and puff is oft but bluff.

Conceit is morally no less meet than is deceit.

To have ought is to be someone. To have nought is to be no one.

To be chronically stressed and distressed is to become depressed.

The female is indispensable, the male incidental.

Woman is care and man is flare.

The female is a well and the male is a dipper.

Satire is flare that does not spare.

To flirt with evil is to be evil.

Ambiguity is ingenuity.

Satirists sate with mockery and hate.

Global inhumanity is global insanity.

Passing time is grief's balm of balms.

Life's pains are life's stains.

Where moderation pales, Absurdia prevails.

Some changes are for the better, others for the worse, and all have
a price tag.

Life has become Venture Capitalism.

Sweat and tears, hopes and fears, wherever and whenever.

Terrorism: not ideality but criminality.

Some faintly smile and quietly toil while others only sit and roil.

To accept is to be accepted, to reject is to be rejected.

Don't grumble when you fumble, or shout when out, just grin and
bear it.

Lies do not right what is wrong.

Wars are not about belief but about power.

When down and out, don't just sit and pout.

To rise when down, just play the clown.

Don't just sit and stare when young and fair.

Hypocrites are society's wily misfits.

Pretence is good defence.

Treasured choice becomes tedious habit.

Procrastination is a temptation that is an abomination.

The sated are never motivated.

The modest are circumspect, the rash but disrespect.

Reach is aspiration, grasp is elation.

Hunting is a thrill, but not for the kill.

A life not lived, leaves no residue.

A measure of leisure and pleasure is meet after any trying bout of toil or trouble.

Wars have had their way, it's time for diplomacy to have its day.

Optimism is explosion and pessimism is implosion.

Life's constants grate and life's changes elate.

The old and common lethargizes, the new and novel energizes.

To procrastinate is to alienate.

To abide folly is to foster folly.

What we are is what we stay.

What you do is what you are.

When the mind meditates, the body hibernates.

Save indeed, and have in need.

Civility oh civility, thou hast become a social casualty.

Integrity, honesty, generosity and civility have become antiquities.

What can break, will break.

Adversity may intimidate or stimulate.

Modesty hampers more than it helps.

Wealth bestows privilege of every ilk.

Wealth has always been a law unto itself.

Money has been both cause and panacea of all too many human wars.

Lies beget wars and wars beget lies.

Money does not whisper.

Reflection enhances perception.

Curiosity kills more rats than cats.

Bribery prevails where most else fails.

Obstacles are adrenalin for some, and anathema for others.

Our tomorrows will ever but differ little from our todays, except
that we mend our ways.

Wealth does not step aside, it shoves.

Work is a trying must and indolence is a pleasant bust.

Curiosity bestirs and indifference besots.

Adversities may intimidate, they can stimulate.

It is easier to be dishonest than it is to be honest.

Eating spurs the appetite.

To be taken with is better than to be taken by.

Spurning learning will leave you yearning.

Pipers demand their price.

To give before you take is to ingratiate.

Most know the self but little, and the other even less.

It never rains but that it pours is a very dour adage.

Indignity is oft but slighted vanity.

Self-adulation has its questionable elation.

Slighted egos and indignation walk hand in hand.

Don't be afraid to be afraid, for your life depends upon it.

Privilege misused is privilege abused.

Aspiration plus inspiration equals salvation.

Women hem and haw and humbly so,
Men are bold and brash and with abandon.

To smile and give is to get and smile.

Malice delights perpetrator and pains recipient.

Too much ventured, too much lost.

A portion of fruit and a portion of vegetables each day will keep
poor health at bay.

Correlation is not causation.

Thing possessions have become thing obsessions.

Wealth divides exasperate, religion divides devastate.

Democracies prescribe, autocracies proscribe.

To persist is to prevail.

Too much gloss is but dross.

To the wanting, little is much, and to the wealthy, much is little.

Ideality is possibility, not reality.

What religions preach is beyond reach.

Politics is a self-serving game, governance is a community-
minded responsibility.

Nothing is isolated, everything is interrelated.

The commonality of humans overshadows the uniqueness of the
individual.

Some faces are open books and others are uncharted maps.

Frustrations are the mother of most deadly aberrations.

Life is a labyrinthian maze that leaves all too many in a
perpetual daze.

Each is a unique continuum from birth to death.

Stasis invites stagnation and change invites consternation.

Some know, more surmise and all too many just guess.

Novelty attracts, the familiar comforts.

Life is a miracle and will remain a mystery.

Good will freely dispensed is always duly recompensed.

There's no recompense for indolence.

Nothing is, but that it is constantly changing.

A good conscience's best for a good night's rest.

What is easily attained is quickly disdained.

To deceive another is to belittle the self.

Common persuasions harmonize, contrary persuasions antagonize.

An e-mail is as public as a postcard.

Life and love are here no less than far afield.

Good will begets good will no less than hostilities beget hostilities.

As long as men prevail, wars will continue without fail.

When women have their way, peace will have its day.

Death is life's most poignant reality.

Our days are numbered but few can count.

Sow and harvest, don't just play and stray.

Women are more fully here than there, men more fully there than here.

In the best of all worlds, givers become receivers and receivers become givers.

One cannot be, but that one first becomes.

Speed reading and slow reading are time, not thought reading.

Individual education is ideality, group education is reality.

Society flirts with ideality and settles for reality.

When you've done your best, you've earned your rest.

Abuses never fail to find their excuses.

'Twas hardly thought, before 'twas wrought.

To toil in vain is to live in pain.

Given mankind's pervasive and persistent gloom and doom, for ought else there's too little room.

The good sedates, the wicked titillates.

Accept with thanks and reject kindly.

Civilities are social responsibilities.

Absolutes are absolutely absurd.

To extend tolerance to the intolerant is to be too tolerant.

All ideologies are ipso facto warped.

It's lonely at the top, and even lonelier at the bottom.

Futility has become a philosophy.

Thought is both blessing and curse.

Indolence deserves no recompense.

To conceive is to receive.

Reflection leads to conception.

To say too much is to say too little.

Every plus drags a minus in its wake.

Judge reality and acclaim ideality.

Too ready rejection of the old and acceptance of the new makes for too much becoming and too little being.

Tolerance unlimited is belief undermined.

Morality deters where deterrence is salutary.

Little is heard when much is said.

To hear is responsive, to listen is deliberate.

To leap high is to fall hard.

'Tis the different that always makes the difference.

More is chance and less is choice.

Needs are fewer than are wants.

The old are generally weary, the young are too often leery, and the middle-aged fumble and bumble as best they can.

Sex and life spell means and end.

Capitalist democracy has well nigh run its course, and socialist capitalism is still too powerless to be born.

All human involvements are psychology-strapped.

A roll in the hay has its price.

A romp on a rump may have a loud consequence.

Freedom is as feared as it is revered.

Jobs that are but jobs demand too much and give too little.

No belief too, is a belief.

Hypocrisy's become a common coin.

Disagree but don't malign.

Memory is recollection and can be correction.

Mortality spells finality but for vain hopes of eternity.

Work can be play and play can be work.

Men and women are of a kind, but not of a mind.

But for fear, many would not be here.

But for otherness, there would be no racism.

Hatred is not time or fuel efficient.

Fight is ever choice, talk an afterthought.

Good will's a gain and ill will's a pain.

Savor both sorrows and joys, they are the stuff of life.

Black is *a problem*, white is *the problem*.

Despair paralyzes, hope surprises.

Adventurers, free spirits, risk takers shake the present and shape the future.

Stoic endurance trumps ostentatious indulgence.

Challenge is the leaven of life.

Let every day be both for work and play.

For the old, the old is the familiar and the familiar is a comfort.

Brains have supplanted brawn.

Sweat and tears breed pioneers.

Piosity smatters of hypocrisy.

Inspiration without perspiration invites exasperation.

But for change, there'd be no past, no future, no time.

To give of one's little is to give of one's self.

Most fear for the self and the fewest fear for others.

To acknowledge another, to aid materially and to bolster in spirit, is to be a sister or a brother.

Soldiers are boys with deadly toys.

Inhumanity is as invasive as humanity is pervasive.

Fame is as fickle as it is elusive.

Where there is life, there is aggression.

Mankind's innate aggressiveness can be attenuated but never extirpated.

Nothing is good or bad, but that it respectively is also bad or good.

Where there is water, there is life.

The sun rises just as surely as it sets.

Where there are shadows, there is light.

Life at strife with life is the nature of life.

Not to know the self is not to know the other.

To know the other is to know the self.

Aggressiveness is life's prevailing proclivity.

Female subtlety irks male prosaicness.

The future is but an admixture of the past, present and novelty.

Christianity's here and hereafter are but flip sides of a coin.

Frivolity, they name is inanity.

Problems are a gift, they give the mind a lift.

A smirk will irk and a grin will win.

Age's afflictions are age's restrictions.

Life's vagaries are inevitabilities.

When testosterone fails, viagra prevails.

The done is ever undone.

Challenges not met, is life not lived.

To taste is to learn to discern.

Life without laughter is itch without scratch.

Sex and money, non plus ultra.

Religion has to be lost before it can be found.

In meditation one loses oneself to find a better self.

Elation and devastation are the children of expectation.

Racism knows little reason and even less compassion.

Balloons inflate slowly and deflate quickly.

Some live reflectively, others live reflexively.

The feckless are never the reckless.

The strong are often wrong and the weak go along.

The unfamiliar path leads to unforeseen possibilities.

The novel becomes the familiar and familiarity breeds contempt.

To others, each is but a walking shade.

Most think little and care even less.

When discussion becomes argument, reason takes wing.

Hypersensitivity is more pain than gain.

Irrationality knows neither reason nor logic.

Rejection thrusts downward or spurs upward.

Each is both more and less than each and others assume to be the case.

To assume the worst of the other is to demean a brother.

Detachment is altercation with, fear of, and flight from.

War has become a world-wide way of life.

When sigh becomes smile, all's well for awhile.

To forgive is to be forgiven.

Absolute certainty is absolute nonsense.

Forbearance and forgiveness have ever been in short supply.

War has become serial soap opera.

Money is no less distractive than it is attractive.

When reach exceeds grasp, what is will last.

Out of sight, out of mind, out of luck.

Every beginning has its end.

Both young and old are enrolled in the school of life.

Life is fight and death is flight.

Life's tumult is followed by death's tranquility.

To be frugal is to be prudent, to be cheap is to be a creep.

Women are taken with children, men are given to sex.

We are in part what life makes of us, and life is in part what we make of it.

To advertize is to spread lies.

The ideal inspires, the real tires.

Virtues are practised not purchased.

Money is means, not substance.

Convention is common practice, not practised truth.

To suffer fools is to invite folly.

Better to suffer than to inflict suffering.

To acknowledge is to respect.

Generosity invites reciprocity.

Feeling is reflex, thought is reaction and action is relief.

Silence can be very telling.

With belief comes solace and relief.

Shadows are darkest when the light is brightest.

The wealthy can be as greedy as the needy.

Masculinity is an asininity.

To be at peace with one's self is happiness itself.

A bad conscience is a good prod.

When sorely discontent, it's broken and not just bent.

Address your stress or suffer even more distress.

Some learn reluctantly, slowly and little, others avidly, quickly and much, but all are the better for it.

Audacity is exciting, caution is boring, and moderation is rewarding.

Fools know all, the wise know limits.

Work and play are flipsides of the same coin.

The mind thinks and fuels, the body does.

Better to give than to get.

To understand is to appreciate.

We learn and teach, then teach and learn.

To lower another to elevate the self is to elevate the other and to lower the self.

Culture, I do fear, is a very thin veneer.

The circumspect act judiciously, the inept react frantically.

The religiously possessed know neither reason nor compassion.

Love is a blind as a bat.

Obsession is a blind fixation.

Humans were fashioned by God and refashioned by the Devil.

Adversity can discourage or encourage further effort.

A hug a day will keep gloom at bay.

Life is lot, culture is venture.

Need is primary and want is secondary.

But for nature and for nurture there would be no future.

The imponderables of life never cease to be pondered.

Women attract and distract, men kill and are killed.

The wise say too little, the foolish too much.

Children are receptive, adults are interceptive.

Those who live to work are obsessed, those who work to live are the blessed.

Jobs are for the hoi polloi, professions for the hoity-toity.

Opportunists abuse opportunity and with impunity.

Education is self and social elevation.

Be thoughtful, be helpful, those helped will be grateful.

One learns from books but more from life.

Love is life's leaven.

Democracy's our ideality, autocracy is our reality.

With consciousness came heaven and hell.

Men stake and take, women share and care.

Though each is a sister or brother, each is as rare as the other.

Challenge tries and taxes, achievement elevates and exhilarates.

Unexpressed expectations are abominations.

Firm faith is true wealth.

Regression of aggression would end oppression.

Heaven *is* what earth *would be*.

A shadowy figure with scythe in hand looms large or small in every life.

Little fails when good will prevails.

Popular piety and conventional thought are everyday fare and not holiday ware.

Epigrams are pithy sayings that please and tease.

Neglect is abuse.

Let live what is alive and let die what cannot survive.

The dead can't talk and the living just gawk.

The united prevail, the discordant fail.

To kill whatever and whyever, is to diminish the self.

Let's remember that every shade of gender is a member of the human kind.

Wars are common recourse and not last resort.

Wars have no winners.

To educate or to train. That is the question.

A little guilt goes a long way for a short time.

Only the valued has any value.

Arrogance is pathological pride.

Beyond unique individuality, each is commonly human.

We come in birth and leave in death, and are left wondering why.

Every attraction is no less distraction.

Virtues are born of goodness, live on in hope, and humanize life.

Too many are too busy doing too little.

Shoes that are not right are shoes that bark and bite.

We know to learn, and we learn to know.

Cats yowl, dogs howl, and humans mumble and grumble.

Jobs tire, callings inspire.

Need spawns beggary and greed spawns usury.

Speed is more compulsion than need.

Risk is more exciting than it is rewarding.

For the timid stasis is refuge, for the bold change is challenge.

Honesty should be carefully selective, lest it become destructive.

Dare with flare and care, don't just grope like a dope and hope.

To live is to think, to do, to hope and to accept.

To be bored is to be boring.

The hunted don't share in the hunter's delight in hunting.

Life's daily struggles take their daily toll.

To be or not to be is the problem.

Silent expectation invites exasperation.

Each is tethered by self and by society.

Perfection is reach, not grasp.

Too many are beyond the reaches of teachers and preachers.

Reflections, like shadows, are reality once removed.

The wealthy are obsessed and the poor are distressed.

When good will pales, turmoil prevails.

Gloves and shoes are not interchangeables.

Men are dogs, women are cats, and children are kids.

Life is a transition from nowhere to nowhere.

Democracy is ever in danger of becoming a mobocracy or a plutocracy.

Character and geography determine a nation's destiny.

Possibility is opportunity and responsibility.

To dare with care is to survive and thrive.

To romance chance makes for a wild dance.

Forethought and afterthought are compass and comfort.

Actions are very telling reflections.

Epigramists are literature's astute minimalists.

Reflection is not an affliction.

Life is reach, not grasp.

Affliction prods reflection.

Possibility is a door waiting to be opened.

Fixed minds are locked doors.

Jeremiads are a valid waste of time.

A smile is contagious, a sneer outrageous.

An open door is an invitation or a suggestion.

We come but to leave and there is no reprieve.

To be of conflicting beliefs is to be of no belief.

Discussion is stimulating, quarrel is agitating.

Teachers are preachers and preachers are teachers, and ne'er the twain shall part.

To burn both ends of the candle is double wear and tear.

Better that hunger be need than want.

To surmise is exploration, not explanation.

The willing and the able are society's makers and shakers.

Capital punishment solves, but fails to resolve.

Good thoughts and good deeds assuage emotional needs.

Nought but humans changed for the better will ever change our
world for the better.

Preachers and teachers are of a kind.

Adversity can be as instructive as it is disruptive.

Globalization is commerce's innovation.

Nationalism guards its boundaries and the corporate ignores all
boundaries.

To be a good parent, one must remain something of a child.

Time *undoes* whatever mankind *does*.

Conscientious application deserves commensurate financial
appreciation.

Beauty is opinion and not inherent quality.

Nerdy boys love their electronic toys.

To educate or to indoctrinate, that is the question.

Human beings are larvae, not butterflies.

Cooperation trumps confrontation.

War is a problem and peace is its solution.

The political world is nation-minded, corporations are
world-focussed.

It's never too late to wipe your slate.

Persuade, don't just invade.

Reciprocity engages, hostility enrages.

Male dominance is female subservience.

War is nothing but guts and gore.

Age can be sage and youth can be uncouth.

Love sates and hate grates.

Humans are plagued and humans do suffer, as was Sisyphus and as did Prometheus.

Indulgence spoils and restraint roils.

Life is a meld of chance and choice.

To give is more rewarding than to take.

Far-away places are like attractive new faces.

Each is a different person to every other person.

For the humble, the weak and the meek, life is but trying and bleak.

Rare is the human not both blessed and blighted.

Nothing is right and nothing is wrong, for everything is both right and wrong.

All is predictable when all is known.

Some do and others don't, some can and others can't, some will and others won't, and nothing is chance or choice.

Affects have their predictable effects.

Exceptionalism maximizes its proponents and minimizes its opponents.

Relativity makes a relative truth of itself.

Subjectivity is reflexive, objectivity is reflective.

—— *Pensive Pauses*

Never to venture is never to fail and never to succeed.

Fate of late seems to love less than to hate.

Civilians taught to love one another and to value life become soldiers taught to hate and to kill.

Grief is ready release and relief.

Exceptions to the rule can change the rule.

Paper print is fading away, electronic print will soon hold sway.

Quarrel can undo some, and redo still others.

To get better, one must first fail.

Mass communication knows no mass intelligence.

Politicians are liberally financed and their patrons are duly romanced.

General equality is an absurdity.

Modesty will not get one from here to there.

Perfection is ideality, imperfection is reality.

Gender bias is as invidious as it is insidious.

Perfectionism makes or breaks.

One person's justification is another person's rationalization.

If little else, quarrel can be cathartic.

Physical size invites surmise.

To rest on one's laurels is to lose one's laurels.

Though of a kind, we fight more than we bind.

To get anywhere, one has to become a go-getter.

Mankind is not good. It but flirts with goodness.

When strong feelings are in command, things quickly get out of hand.

Life is more than that which meets the eye.

Go-getters are our pace-setters.

Minimum government for the haves, maximum for the have-nots.

Bark but don't growl or bite.

Do it or rue it.

Pickpockets are slicks not hicks.

Choice is burdened by responsibility.

Mankind's plethora of existential questing defies all answers.

Freedom from what and for what? That is the question.

Serious thought leaves too many very distraught.

When myth pales, religion fails.

Time and memory distill what was the present.

The present become the past is a trove that long will last.

The timid are aggressive in their passive way.

Aggression is life's most common expression.

But for heights we would know no depths and but for depths we would know no heights.

Comprehension invites compassion.

To do nothing is to do something.

Love is many different things to many different folks.

Apprehension invites condescension.

The best are capable of the worst, and the worst are capable of the best.

Human beings are commonly sinners, rarely saints.

To be at a loss for words is to have time for thought.

Boys will be boys, but then are men.

While all do age, but few become sage.

Women are given to cradles and men are taken with cars.

What evolves and flourishes will devolve and perish.

Nothing is, but that it's ever changing.

To rest on one's laurels is to lose one's laurels.

Physical stature can be imposing, mental prowess can be disclosing.

The female epitomizes life, the male epitomizes the incidental.

The old is venerable and the new is celebrated.

Nothing is ever as final as never.

The female cherishes and nurtures, the male challenges and battles.

The world's masters are few, its servants many.

Eating three times a day is more cultural than natural.

Wastrels and ne'er-do-wells have always gone their way and have always had their day.

Civility makes for tranquility.

To appease is not to solve but to please.

Where there's life, there's aggression, and where there's aggression, there's life.

Dejection follows on the heels of rejection.

The truths of metaphysics are no less tentative than those of science.

Eternity knows neither beginning nor end and is itself quite unknowable.

The universe was never born of a cosmic explosion. It was never born and will never die.

Everything that ever was, is and will be, will ever change and ever be.

An angry mind is a mind that is blind.

Too little love can devastate, too much love can asphyxiate.

Entrepreneurs are wooers not doers.

Sloppy garb and sloppy thought walk hand in hand.

The poor are burdened by poverty, the rich are burdened by wealth.

War has become one of life's major constants.

Attractions are no less distractions.

When thinking, feeling and acting selves are in sync, life is really in the pink.

Each is as no other ever was, and as no other will ever be.

Shame can be a badge of honor or a badge of dishonor.

Stress and distress of whatever ilk are always good cause for a reflective pause.

A good conscience is a good measure of one's pleasure.

Care and help are rare and spare.

Thanks to muscle memory, the human body can self-function.

Better to play fair and lose than to cheat and win.

Better to lament than to resent.

Excite, yes, but don't incite.

The word crapulence is not as redolent as it sounds.

Procrastination is good cause for provocation.

The different have always had more than their fair share of
differences.

To be rash and brash is to court rejection and dejection.

Fools bloviate while wise men meditate.

In a world peopled only by dwarfs, there would be no dwarfs.

One person's cold becomes another person's pneumonia.

Terrorism, like all other extremes, is born of desperation.

Hatred in all its manifestations is mankind's sin of sins.

Education enlightens, training fashions skills.

Men are manic, women know restraint.

Truths are truths and facts are facts and ne'er the twain should meet.

Hate poisons what it touches.

If they know not better, teach them better.

When morality becomes a casualty, society pays a penalty.

The crooked road is more profitable than the straight.

Venality knows no propriety.

Justice fails where vengeance prevails.

Desegregation is ideal theory, segregation is actual fact.

Sex, food and money are popular preoccupations.

To listen is to be heard.

When things go wrong, the strong will fight and the weak take flight.

The dead are not dead until they are out of one's head.

Nature knows neither haste nor waste.

What is culturally embraced today is culturally effaced tomorrow.

The right is known, the wrong is done.

Crime attracts more than punishment deters.

Culture embraces questionably and culture rejects questionably.

Prison is less deterring than crime is rewarding.

Poverty perpetuates poverty.

Much is done and then undone, and no less enthusiastically.

The death penalty for crime is itself a crime.

Chronic complaint is more pathology than remedy.

Nervous Nellies have queasy bellies.

To aid those in need is a good act indeed.

Revenge is sweet, chocolate is sweeter.

Better to choose to amuse than to choose to abuse.

To brook fools is to be a fool.

Vengeance, though sweet, is not meet.

Retaliation invites retaliation.

Catholicism embraced and absorbed, Protestantism reflected and rejected.

Women have found themselves and a voice that resonates.

To give more is, forsooth, to get more.

Run both to be fit and to have fun.

The young are fresh and frisky and the old fret and frown.

Neither old nor new is always better.

Better to stand for something than just to stand.

We preach and we teach, we try and we cry.

Moderation in all matters, of common sense smatters.

To hunt and kill for a thrill, is to hunt and kill for nil.

The daffy and the silly can be right dilly.

Over-production and over-consumption are born of greed and
not need.

Theculturallyoldisfadingfast,andtheculturallynewisn'tyetinview.

It's such a waste to argue style and taste.

To shilly-shally or to dilly-dally is to fumble and jumble.

Humanism is our yesterday, technology is our today.

Automate, then hibernate.

Treasure life for what is is, and not for what it could be.

To come to grips and to terms with self and life is to do what all
too few are actually able to do.

To flatter is to sweetly chatter.

To be relished, it has to be embellished.

POEMS

Read slowly and with care,
Concur or issue take,
And then your own poems pen.

The Choice is Yours

Don't rant and rave,
Don't whine and grumble,
Don't weep and wail.

Don't leer and sneer,
Don't tease and taunt,
Don't lie and cheat,
Don't denigrate and humiliate.

Don't sit and stare,
Don't rush and tumble,
Don't wait and wonder.

Life's not as bad as you may think,
Humans are your kindred beings,
And mindful action is yours to take,
It's up to you and up to me!

Achievement

Achievement of whatever ilk,
Be it modest or impressive,
Is a social badge of honour:
It invigorates and elevates
And bolsters respect and self-esteem,
Due reward for honest effort!

Dolendum est!

We once were four,
Four lively branches in the wind,
Are that no more.

We're now but three,
Three frail branches withered and old,
And wondering when.
Such is life!

The Choice is Yours and Mine

The Physical
We are weak and frail,
Life is struggle and pain,
Such are our givens, our lot.

The Mental
We have a mind and will,
And where there's thought and resolve
Our givens need not prevail.

The choice is yours and mine,
Now act and do not whine!

Being

With the wind we come
And with the wind we go,
Where, whither and why
Is not for us to know.

To account in learned thought,
In science, philosophy, religion,
Is quite beyond our reach,
All words and no precision.

Ours is not to know,
But to accept and live,
To become what we can be,
To learn what can be learned,
To do what can be done,
To live long and right fully,
In time, content to go.

With the wind we come
And with the wind we go,
And why we'll never know,

But twixt the come and go,
Life is ours to live,
To do with as we choose.

In Memoriam

A spirited lass she was
Strong-minded and quite fearless.
A beauty she became,
Admired and much pursued.

Able and resourceful,
She went her chosen way
And did her chosen things,
Content and full of zeal.

Her very humble background
Taught her diligence,
Left her penny wise
Yet generous to a fault.

She was no one's fool,
Knew her mind right well
Firmly stood her ground,
With rarely a trace of malice.

A mother hen she became,
Protective of her brood
And no less of her man.
They knew to whom to turn.

For ninety years and some,
Mary Mileck Sharp
Graced this world of ours,
And now that she has left,
As too all must in turn,
We are the poorer for it.

Ave atque vale.

The Blues

Grief for Goethe was not rare,
To wallow in it, he did not care.

Aug', mein Aug', was sinkst du nieder?
Goldne Träume, kommt ihr wieder?
Weg, du Traum! so Gold du bist;
Hier auch Lieb' und Leben ist.

The poetry of these four lines
Is surely lost in their translation.
Their thought suffers less in its migration.

Eyes, my eyes, wherefore so downcast,
Again beset by golden dreams?
Away o dream, fair though you are,
Here too there is both love and life.

Advice

Goethe was a student of life
And ever given to wise advice.

Willst du immer weiter schweifen?
Sieh', das Gute liegt so nah.
Lerne nur das Glück ergreifen,
Denn das Glück ist immer da.

My English rendering of these lines
Is just in matter, less so in form.

Do you always yearn for elsewhere?
Take heed, the good is ever nigh.
Learn but good luck to grasp and hold,
For good fortune's ever here.

Love and Music

For German Romantics of yore,
Love and music were wed.

Liebe spricht in Tönen,
Denn Gendanken sind zu fern.

This meld of love and music
Finds ready expression in English.

Music is love's language,
For thought is too remote.

Pantheism

The writer Goethe, like Spinoza the philosopher,
An omnipresent deity embraced.

Was wär ein Gott, der nur von aussen stiesse,
Im Kreis das All am Finger laufen liesse.
Ihm ziemt's die Welt im Innern zu bewegen,
Sich in Natur, Natur in sich zu hegen,
So dass, was in ihm lebt und webt und ist
Nie seinen Geist, nie seine Kraft vermisst.

Rendered in rhymeless English this would be:

Of what import a God who stands apart,
Allowing all to but spin at his finger tips,
More fitting he move the world internally,
That he and nature, each in the other, flourish,
So that everything that he comprises,
Neither its essence nor strength will ever lose.

Mentor Goethe

Wise old Goethe
Liked to caution,
And curt indeed
He could be.

Feiger Gedanken,
Bängliches Schwanken,
Weibliches Klagen,
Ängstliches Zagen,
Wendet kein elend,
Macht dich nicht frei.

Allen Gewalten
Zum Trutz sich erhalten
Kräftig sich zeugen,
Nimmer sich beugen,
Rufet die Arme
Der Götter herbei.

In fair English,
Rhymeless though
And somewhat gauche,
This verse would be:

Cowardly thought,
Timid indecision,
Female complaint,
Anxious hesitation,
All counters no misery
And breaks no fetters.

Against all forces
Stand stubbornly firm,
Show yourself strong,
Ne'er bend or yield.
This will assure
The help of the Gods.

Cultures Go and Cultures Come

A culture in decline slips slowly
Beyond the pale of right and wrong.
Social knots once tied with zeal
Loosen slowly, then unravel
Till all's again a primal mass.
Now nothing's right and nothing's wrong,
Everything's right and everything's wrong,
The ugly's beautiful and the beautiful's ugly,
The good is bad and the bad is good,
And what is true and false is choice.

Humans, frantically giddy and confused,
Will both mourn and rejoice in this morass
Until they've had their fill of formlessness,
Until they thirst again for light and guidance.
New prophets and messiahs will then sprout
And preach and spread new possibilities.
One, as was the case with Jesus Christ,
With Muhammed, Buddha and Confucius,
Will emerge triumphant, and his gospel
Will become the core of yet another culture.

Cultures bud and grow, flourish and flower,
Slowly wilt and wither, then pass away.
Such is their evolution, such is their lot.

The Western World's Judeo-Christian culture
Has reached its twilight stage, is well-nigh spent,
And the World of Islam's close behind.

Sic gloriae mundi veniunt atque transeunt!

Two and Two is Four

When consumers spend too much,
The commercial world profits too much,
And all peaks in inflation.

When consumers spend too little,
The commercial world profits too little,
And all ends in stagnation.

When consumers spend moderately,
The commercial world profits moderately,
And all remains quite stable.

Two and two is four, no less, no more,
A lesson easily learned but rarely heeded.
Extremes have always beckoned and prevailed,
And moderation's never been temptation.

The Spirit and the Flesh

Christ was born of the spirit.
He fed the many,
Raised from the dead,
Died for the living
And then joined God in Heaven.

Humans are born of the flesh.
They know but the self,
Vie with each other,
Leave dead in their wake,
Then long to end in heaven.

No end to Chutzpah!

There is a Time for Everything

Where there's a will
There is a way,
Is an adage
Not always in sway.

The older males get,
The more they lust,
But it's all futile,
For though will's strong,
The flesh, with age,
Is frail and meek.

There's a moral
To this sad fact:
Spring's the time
For sowing,
Autumn's meant
For reaping.

Do in spring,
In autumn rest.
Let all follow
As night, the day.

Dusk

The body's become quite frail
And the mind's begun to fail.
What once was is no more
And soon we'll be but lore.
C'est dommage,
Mais c'est la vie!

The Being I am

Touch me not
Where you were wont to.
It discomforts,
Leaves me too tense,
Quite unresponsive.

What once was thrill
No longer is.
Time has changed
My body's needs,
My mind's desires.

Every flower
Its season has,
More treasured, too,
Its passing bloom.
Give thanks for that.

Touch me not
Where you were wont to,
But do love me
And do cherish
The being I am!

What Next?

Sunset is at hand,
Twilight's fading fast.
The day a long toil was,
What has night to offer?

I can only guess!

Too Much Too Fast

Few are the bonds
That yet remain
To bind me
To what is.

Too many roads,
Too many bridges
For me to travel,
For me to cross.

The country lane,
The twisting trail
Were mine to travel,
Mine to know.

Change has become a whirl,
Life has become a maze,
I'm left baffled,
Estranged and dazed.

Sic transit gloria

America has seen better days,
Everything seems to have gone awry.

Our political world's in disarray,
Our foreign policy's been disastrous.

Our materialism and consumerism,
Blindly indifferent to loftier things,
Have spawned a lowly shopping culture.

Our passionate embrace of whatever freedoms,
Unqualified and unmindful of consequences,
Has made license and weapon of Freedom.

Our individualism and capitalism,
Self-indulgent and short-sighted
And oblivious of the commonweal,
Have left a shameful growing divide
Twixt wanting many and wealthy few
And made a plutocracy of our democracy.

Our security, a rightful concern,
Has become a rank obsession,
A wily pretext for decisive action,
For costly serial wars abroad,
Empire-minded expansionism
That can end but in disaster.

America was once an envied nation,
A country of wealth, of law and order,
A refuge for the world's downtrodden,
A country worthy of emulation.
Such it was but is no more.
Thanks for hubris and to folly.

Life's Wanting

We humans are a restless kind,
We are an ever wanting breed.
Want more of all that gives us pleasure,
Want less of everything that pains.

We want more wealth, we want less struggle,
Want more leisure, want less pressure,
Want more brain, want less challenge,
Want more joy, want less grief.

There is no end to human wanting,
Wise acceptance's a rare bird.
Wanting is an ingrained bane,
Wanting's the very core of life!

Life's Twilight

He sits alone,
Is given to thought and sentiment.

He tends to his garden.
Communes in silence with nurtured plants.

He repairs to his study,
To read, to think and to write dirges.

He strolls past homes,
In thought recalls who once dwelled there.

He dines apart,
Chews slowly and is vaguely pensive.

He retires at night,
Revisits what was, in restless sleep.

Still present he is, yet ever less of what there is,
More given to distant past than to the here and now.
He lingers on and waits for the approaching end,
Mourning what he's lost and fearing what's to come.

Life's twilight is a very trying time for most,
When coming to terms with self and life becomes all urgent,
When existential aloneness becomes acutely painful,
When lament, regret, dread and despair are overwhelming,
When time's too short to make amends and to atone,
When anxiety and gloom become a stifling pall.

But for a blessed few, life's twilight is ordeal,
An ordeal quite in accord with life's harsh road and ways.

Thinkers and Doers

There are our sensitive thinkers,
Then, too, our hardier doers.
Thinkers think and rarely do,
Doers do and rarely think.
Such it is, a pity too.

More ideal too, and more productive,
If our thinkers and our doers
Were both to think and both to do.
Each a fuller being would be,
The world also the better for it.

Goethe was of like persuasion,
He summed it up more curtly too:
To think and to do,
To do and to think,
The epitome of all wisdom is.

Our Culture of Things

Ours is a very material culture,
A world of transiently attractive things,
Novelty's the order of the day
And boredom belongs to yesteryear.

Ours is a world of electronic things,
Of brilliant devices that lure and trap,
A culture given to object attachment
More than to human preoccupation.

The Electronics Age is a deviation,
A passion for things and not for humans,
A seduction that has been irresistible
And for it we're both more and less.

The Good and the Bad

For some, indeed for far too many humans,
The bad has always been a secret passion.
The forbidden, unlike the touted good,
Seems ever to have been a fascination,
Acted upon by some, just fancied by others.
Among the latter was Hugo von Hoffmannsthal,
Austrian poet of the late 19th century.
A memorable couplet of his attests to this:
"Eintönig ist das Gute, schal und bleich,
Allein die Sünde ist unendlich reich."

These polished lines could in wan English read:
The good is insipid, pale and tedious,
The sinful alone is rich beyond all bounds.

Life's a composite of taxing binaries,
Of moral musts and contrary inclinations.
Such is life, such our human lot.
The choice is ours, as too its consequences.
C'est la vie!

Two Paths

You came my way,
I'm glad you did.
We're both the better for it.

The years slipped by,
We slowly melded,
And are the richer for it.

To chance we owe
Much thanks and more,
That our two paths did merge.

Vive la Différence

Nations are a motley lot
and idiosyncratic too,
Each is rightly-wrongly branded
and permanently too.

Americans are money-minded
and given to sport and fast-food.
Germans are very law-abiding
and much committed to work.
Frenchmen treasure their leisure time
and love to wine and die.
Italians are lively social creatures
and flout authority.
Spaniards are suave and volatile
and prize their bulls they do.
Russians are soulful country bumpkins
and vodka's their cure of cures.
Englishmen are staid and proper
and love their past and pomp.
The Swiss are bank- and mountain-minded
and neutrality's their game.

Nations are a motley lot
and idiosyncratic too.
Each country has its telling features
and each is smugly proud.

Our Sense of Sight

One can see what is alive,
One can also see what's dead,
But life itself's beyond our view
And death's no specter for our eyes.

What's spawned by love is clear to see,
As is no less what's wrought by hate,
But love itself's beyond description
And hate has yet to come in sight.

A deed of courage is a joy to see,
An act of cowardice pains the eyes,
But eyes on courage cannot feast
And to cowardice eyes are blind.

Smell and taste we can and do,
Sound we hear and touch enjoy,
But smell and taste, sound and touch
Are all abstractions beyond our sight.

Of our complex world of senses,
Sight is our most treasured gift,
Limited though it is to tangibles
And dependent though it is on light.

A Reminder

Life is a precious miracle,
Live it fully.
Love is a blessed bond,
Nurture it warmly.
Adversity is a challenge,
Meet it boldly.
Death is a final act,
Accept it calmly.

Time's Flow

Three choice children were my lot,
Each quite different from the other,
Each a source of pride and joy,
And for that I'm deeply thankful.

Grandchildren three did come my way,
Again two boys and but one girl,
Without whom life would be right bare.
I count my blessings night and day.

And should I linger on much longer,
Another precious mix may follow.
Should God choose to so oblige,
My cup would spill with gratitude.

Time's flow will tell!

Such it is

The past is fading,
The present's ailing,
And future holds no promise.

Such are the lives,
And such the woes
Of almost all the old.

There's nought can change,
And nothing end
This agony of being.

Accept we must,
Accept we can,
And smiling go our way.

Bridges and Walls

Bridges and open doors,
Walls and shuttered windows,
The former invite and unite,
The latter bar and ban.

People have their barriers,
And too their welcome mats,
Of the former far too many,
Of the latter far too few.

The unknown is suspect,
Poses threat, stirs fear.
The known spawns trust and comfort,
And each has consequences.

Never truly to know
Is ever to be on guard,
To opt for protective walls,
And not for friendly bridges.

Nations are no different,
They too exclude in fear.
 Bridges are the answer,
And walls persistent woe.

Epitomes

Epitomes are more than legion.
Every noun's a superlative
Of whatever you choose to think,
Evidencing a mode of thought
And revealing a private scale of beliefs.

Life is the miracle of miracles,
Love is the emotion of emotions,
Empathy is the bond of bonds,
Regret is the futility of futilities.

Death is the finality of finalities,
Hate is the scourge of scourges,
Lie is the deception of deceptions,
Apology is the formality of formalities.

Heaven is the reward of rewards,
Hell is the punishment of punishments,
Peace is the blessing of blessings,
War is the blight of blights.

Religion is the solace of solaces,
Music is the panacea of panaceas,
Truth is the elusive of elusives,
Pain is the agony of agonies.

Sight is the bliss of blisses,
Thought is the wonder of wonders,
Hearing is the drama of dramas,
Imagination is the flight of flights.

This could go on ad nauseam
For there's no end to epitomes.
The point's been made, enough is enough,
What might trail is yours to shape.

It's Time

Now that but mowing the garden lawn
Has come to be a trying chore,
It's become very painfully obvious
That my days of action are spent
And that it's time to spare the limbs,
Time for more reflective observation
And time for more intensive introspection.

Acceptance

The past is fading,
The present is paling,
The future holds no promise.

Such sentiment
Is but lament,
Tells more of self than life.

Best to embrace
And not deface,
And be the richer for it.

More Sad than Mad

I'm saddened when I reflect upon mankind:
Saddened by the prevalent hostility
That characterizes the relationships of nations;
Saddened by the prevalent factionalism
That ever plagues most nations internally;
Saddened by the prevalent animosities
That ever mar most personal relationships;
Saddened by the dearth of common sense
That characterizes the human community.

To which the French would say, "mais c'est la vie."

Few Choose to Heed

Where there's soil and seed,
Where sun and rain,
There is hope and promise.

Where there's brotherhood,
Where love, goodwill,
There is hope and promise.

Where there's fear and hate,
Where violence,
There's no hope or promise.

Few choose to comprehend,
To see, to heed.
Most go their hopeless way!

A Pity

Maidens lithe and comely
become
Matrons stiff and homely
and
Young men strong and handsome
become
Old oafs weak and withered.
A Pity.
The wear and tear of time!

Imponderables

We cannot see life,
Can only see the living.
We cannot see death,
Can only see the dead.

Neither can be measured,
Nor even touched or felt.
Life, no less than death,
Is but a quality.

Qualities, no more,
Of all organic matter
That chances to spring alive,
Only, in time, to die.

How matter's animated,
Is quite beyond our ken.
Its rise to consciousness,
Is equal mystery.

Life's a murky miracle,
Death's its partner end.
Humans know of both,
But can only muse and wonder.

Freedom Abused

America's a country of serious thought,
Of think tanks, universities,
Of science and technology,
Of creative entrepreneurs.

America's a mecca of make-believe,
Of Hollywood and Disneyland,
Of glamour, flimflam, tinsel and sham,
Of amusement, raucous mirth ad nauseam.

America's a land of enormous wealth,
Of expansive forests and fertile plains,
Of mines, oil and industries,
Of more than enough for everyone.

America's a land of poverty,
Of millions who live from hand to mouth,
Of a plethora of homeless people,
Of needed food stamps, welfare checks.

America's a country of grave divides,
Divides that make for chronic turmoil
The gap between the white and black
Has closed but little in recent years.
Anti-Semitism, once very public,
Simmers strongly on in private.
In our land of the free, illegals
Are freely maltreated and exploited.
The religious and the non-religious
Are each dismissive of the other.
America's peaceniks and warmongers
Are at loggerheads as ever.
The pros and cons of gun control
Have left deep rancor in their wake.

Private and nationalized medical care
Have left two camps in bitter strife.
A deep split in the political world
Has badly impaired the country's governance.
A chasm separates the monied few
From the many with their less.
These and other national divides
Have left America in chronic disarray!

How to account for this fractured whole,
This country roiled by controversy,
This land that knows no commonweal,
This enigma that is America?

One major single cause would be
America's romance with liberty!
Freedom, America's crowning glory,
The basis of its very being,
The right that trumps all other rights,
Ironically became America's undoing:
The god-given right to live freely and happily,
Legally enshrined by its founding fathers,
But constitutionally left unqualified,
Became unbridled freedom of expression,
Unfettered individualism and license,
And America's commonweal,
Too little stressed in the constitution,
Became a matter of little concern.

Had America's founding fathers
Focussed more on the common good,
Dwelt more on liberty's vital restraints,
Most of the country's above divides
Would never have seen the light of day.

Liberty, like all precious rights,
Is hard-won and very vulnerable,
Easily corrupted and quickly lost,
And the result is socially devastating.

To right what went wrong in America,
Freedom must be born anew,
A freedom that knows limits and restraints,
A freedom mindful of the whole
And no less than of the part.
A freedom disciplined and reflective.

The challenge is clear, imperative.
Will America rise to the occasion?

EPIGRAMS

Epigrams are challenge, not conversion.

*N*ot to appreciate is not to be appreciated.

Lies begin when pens begin to scratch.

Authors are skillful writers and highly imaginative liars.

Pity is poison, empathy is balm.

Compromise is expediency and not ideality.

Anarchy is liberty without responsibility.

Curb your want and heed your need.

To become expedient has become expedient.

Mourn quietly, wail if you must.

Pity is agreeable, sympathy is commendable and empathy is laudable.

Life is a dance born of chance.

Belief affords relief and doubt spawns grief.

Work can be play and play can be work.

Hills that are long and steep, challenge the legs and feet.

Politics and idealism mix like oil and water.

Fabrication is work, imitation is talent, and creation is genius.

Many a pastime has gradually become an all-time passion.

Speeches not brief and to the point, invite noses out of joint.

Chronic indignation invites chronic indigestion.

Money is not the measure of one's worth.

The adventurous initiate, the cautious regulate.

To expect as little as possible is to be as little disappointed
   as possible.

Great minds seed, lesser spirits feed.

Indignation upsets, resignation resets.

Those in the know counter the popular flow.

Originality is a rare and prized commodity.

Indignation tempts termination, resignation invites conservation.

Anarchy is absolute liberty and absolute liberty precludes liberty.

Work is play for some, and for others, play is work.

Romantic love is very chimerical, sexual love is very physical.

Humans feel reflexively and think reluctantly.

Humor's leaven is a treasured touch of heaven.

Life we berate and death we hate.

Materialism and consumerism are the life blood of capitalism.

Theory is tidy, practice is messy.

Too many promises remain but promises.

Life is trying temporality and death is painful finality.

Education broadens, training sharpens.

To remember is to appreciate, to learn and to grow and to
   experience is to appreciate, to learn and to grow.

The adult was a child and the child will be an adult.

A world of gadgetry can end in a cultural tragedy.

Religions have been mankind's heaven and hell.

Possibility is boredom's knell.

Gods are born when needed and die when no longer heeded.

A sage assuages, a fool enrages.

Sport is both exhilarating and debilitating.

To win can be to lose and to lose can be to win.

Trivial recreation knows no moderation.

Amnesty is a touch of humanity.

To test another's patience is to invite another's wrath.

Better to be full of oneself than to be empty.

Jeremiads deflate and eulogies inflate.

Those who aim and strain to please, manage ably to displease.

To try one's limits is to test one's strength.

To be full of oneself is to be empty otherwise.

Possessions tend to possess their possessors.

Money is no less pain than it is gain.

Obsessions are regressions.

Empathy is intimate, pity is aloof.

Flattery is sweet chicanery.

Retaliation is reciprocity, not solution.

Perception is all too often deception in need of correction.

Believe what you will, but do what you morally should.

Reciprocity is geniality, retaliation is hostility.

Yes, you can, you need but try.

Fallowed fields promise better yields.

To live life fully is to embrace death contentedly.

A clear head, kind heart and busy hands are enough to meet life's
many demands.

Work and dignity walk hand in hand.

Money has no scruples.

The known invites, the unknown intrigues.

Security stimulates, insecurity agitates.

To exercise is to energize.

Serious addictions are deadly afflictions.

Insecurity knows no tranquility.

Gambling is a money-making racket, not a money-winning game.

Arrogance is bark not bite.

To remember the past is to be mindful of the future.

What sorrow and tears commemorate, time will surely obliterate.

Being is an inexorable becoming.

Figures of speech are to language what ornaments are to a
Christmas tree.

Arrogance is offensive pose and pretence.

Pomposity is pretentious loquacity.

Bombast is hoity-toity ballast.

Fiction is invention not fact or lie.

Hands once broke our bread, knives now slice instead.

Partiality grates and impartiality ingratiates.

Futility is inability to see any possibility.

Time takes its toll, commented a youthful wayfarer to a wizened old farmer.

Practised thought invites practised action.

Not to heed the past is to imperil the future.

When things go wrong, children will whimper, mothers sob, and fathers curse.

Temptation is as common as it is compelling.

Thought can distraught.

Revenge does not resolve.

Procrastination is evasion not recuperation.

Disagreement need not be disagreeable.

Not to heed is to bleed.

To be defensive can be offensive.

Generosity should not be a curiosity.

To shortchange is to estrange.

The strong may be wrong and the slight may be right.

Like the beyond, earth is heaven and hell.

Water slakes thirst, food sates hunger, and curiosity rouses the mind.

Anger quickly roused should be quickly doused.

While the devil smirks, God beholds His flock and frowns.

The cheery should be a little leery.

Eccentricities can be amusing curiosities.

The fastidious can be hideous.

Anger, like fire, burns to its own destruction.

Nothing comes of nothing.

Contentment thaws, resentment claws.

To be content with the self is to be a peace with the self.

To become too heavily invested in material things, is to become too arrested humanly.

Fear is a commodity that has never lacked sellers and buyers.

Reality and perception go their separate ways.

Success is earned not bought.

Fools tolerate their follies.

Success inflates and failure deflates.

Fools are fools no matter where they may repair.

Hearsay is meresay not factsay.

All's but relative, all's but view, and that's not new.

The weak are meek and the strong know no wrong.

To denigrate another is to belittle the self.

After labor, rest you'll savor.

Competition enhances ability, it also spawns animosity.

It takes no breaks to make mistakes.

Not to understand is to strand.

Lust if you must, but leave it at that.

Romance was once a courting dance. Today, lust has its at once way.

Much that is, all too soon will no more be.

Technology has become today's theology.

Gods have ever been, are, and will ever be.

The family is, but soon will go its way.

Education has had its day, training now holds sway.

The Western World's factories have gone East, and the Eastern World's religions have gone West.

Mankind has ever needed and wanted and will ever need and want.

Men, like cocks, have long ruled the roost, and women, like queen bees, will soon control the hive.

Men want to take and women want to be taken.

Fences attract gawkers.

The dead talk but are not heeded.

Dance is romance on display.

Rights are loud and responsibility is shy.

Song and dance enhance romance.

We can't get along without dance and song.

All countries have their unique songs and dances.

Dogs bark and cats meow, men grumble and women whine.

Some individuals are but anecdotes or short stories, others are fairytales or musicals, still others are poetry or drama, and but a few are grand majestic novels.

Fight if you must, flee if you can.

Understand before you command.

Song and dance are born of joy, and are a joy.

The helpless are hopeless and the hopeless are helpless.

Emotions out of control invite commotions beyond control.

Better a slap in the face than a pat on the head.

A hug and smile will never rile.

Gender deviations are normalities, not abnormalities.

Song and dance make for romance.

Male and female are more alike than dislike.

Oh, to but both know and comprehend.

Flesh is fact, spirit is faith.

Day and night are but the presence and absence of light.

Such as good and bad are moralities, not realities.

To understand is to be less judgmental.

Nothing comes of nothing.

To be judgmental is to have a bee in one's bonnet.

Consolidation's strong, fragmentation's weak.

Persist and prevail, or give up and fail.

Relent and repent before you are spent.

Persist or desist, that is the question.

It is banal to be anal.

To understand is to stay one's hand.

Better to adore than to deplore.

Here but for a spell, then heaven or hell.

Rapacity knows little moderation and even less sagacity.

The homeless and jobless are society's helpless and hopeless.

Deities are more necessities than pieties.

Abundancy breeds profligacy.

To be outstanding is to be deified or vilified.

Rapacity has boundless ability.

Religions are palliative afflictions.

To go one's way is to go away.

To rage chronically is to age perceptively.

The wily do not wile away their time.

Wit and grit are always a hit.

The old and bent are cold and spent.

A mother will smother, a father will hover.

Courtship is thrill and tumult, marriage is tumult and thrill.

To emote is to impress, to reason is to express.

Wise it is to think and to do, and to do and to think.

Mankind's many bibles have been balm and bulwark.

For many, death's an ominous reaper, for some, a cordial
receptionist.

See and say, don't be blind and dumb.

The nature of a country's cultural DNA determines the nature of
its cultural evolution.

For the prudent, exigencies are priorities.

The heedy rarely become needy.

Money has become poison and panacea.

Too much, too readily available, obfuscates rather than elucidates.

To assess the past is to shape the future.

Not to know is not to care.

Opulence is but extravagant appearance.

To feel old is to be old.

Hyperbole impresses more than it expresses.

Life is but a visit, not a stay.

Describe we can, explain we can't.

Self-righteousness and self-delusion are of a kind.

Life never ceases to appeal and to repel.

To understand an enemy is to make a friend.

Instrument and player become a meld of melodious sound.

To end friction is to begin interaction.

To think but not to do, or to do but not to think, is to be and not to be.

Not to answer, is an answer.

Bed and table life enable.

Perception is ever in need of correction.

Intuition is inclination, not inspiration.

To debate is to argue and not to elucidate.

Argument rends more than it mends.

Peace of mind is hard to find.

Books are a pleasure, and pleasure is a treasure.

Friendships are the best of human relationships.

To know is to know better.

Friendships wear well, relationships fare poorly.

To know more is to grow more.

To have ought is to be ought and to have nought is to be nought.

Forgiveness is future-minded, not past-bound.

Life is a struggle for one and all, sweet at times and often bitter.

Too many have too little and too many have too much.

The fortunate are few, the unfortunate are many.

The few know, the many think they know.

The body's needs trigger its appetites.

Wants feed greed.

Much that is valued has no intrinsic value.

Too much argument is beside the point.

Exploitive and oppressive relationships are intrinsic to capitalism.

The hungry will hunger on despite the earth's plenty.

Accountants tend to be poker-faced and straight-laced.

To heed another's need is to win another's heart.

Oblige requests and be grateful for bequests.

Enough is never enough.

With all its bread and honey, heaven needs no leaven.

Freedom unqualified is freedom denied.

The poor struggle to make it, the rich stack it.

Nothing is exclusively right or wrong.

The past is a shadow, the present a glare and the future a glimmer.

Some mature and others just age.

As the old become more numerous, the past becomes more present.

When reason and logic cease to be involved, thought ceases to evolve.

Some are so given to the moment that past and future are of no moment.

Hunters are children given to a deadly game.

Religion is packaged belief, philosophy is labor of love.

Yesteryear's abnormals are rapidly becoming today's normals.

The tolerance of intolerance should not be tolerated.

You should have your say, but may or may not have your way.

Human beings are restlessly creative and no less restlessly destructive.

Evanescence is life's only permanence.

Beauty is a fickle figment of the imagination.

Marriage was something, is something, and will become yet something else.

Hate takes much and gives nothing.

Some people are volatile, others labile, and still others are but bumps on a log.

Romance, like every other song and dance, is but a passing chance.

Unfettered capitalism made a plutocracy of America's treasured democracy.

Gambling is a perilous dance of chance.

Capitalistic democracy, No; democratic capitalism, Yes.

No judge can, or should be, absolutely objective.

War, a traditional option, should never be an option.

Wishful thinking is vain thinking.

To flatter is to pave the road for license.

Diplomacy does what ultimata can't.

For some work is play, and for others play is work.

Men are on the prowl, and women lurk nearby.

Leisure is a measure of one's pleasure.

Knowledge is effort and wisdom is grace.

Impulse buyers are ready liars.

Not to try is never to know.

Shout if you must, but never strike.

Men chase and women lure.

To praise is to raise, to upbraid is to degrade.

The fat are rarely fleet on their feet.

Children do, grownups plan and plot.

Some are nimble of mind, others of body, and still others of both
or of neither.

Children tend to be spontaneous, and adults are inclined to be
devious.

Optimists sport their rose-colored glasses, and pessimists are
wedded to their blinders.

Obedience is all too often but a convenience.

The hoity-toity would be the epitome of propriety.

The right are convinced that they are right, but so are the wrong.

The weak Jims would be strong Johns.

The hoity-toity has its arts and the hoi polloi its sports.

Art at its best is a meld of genius and grace.

When each of a pair serves the purposes of the other, all is well and fair.

Humans are neither thinkers nor feelers, but thinking feelers or feeling thinkers.

War leaves only losers in its wake.

The living keep the dead alive.

Yesterday is gone, today is grin and bear it, and tomorrow is smile and hope.

Death is ebb not flow.

The beyond is beyond human ken.

We know that we do not know, but don't believe it.

Imprecision characterizes all human communication.

Law of the jungle has become law of the land.

What is alive is determined to remain alive, come hell or high water.

All is ultimately in vain, for nothing that is, will ever remain.

Humans may pray and flay, but that ghostly reaper cannot be held at bay.

The world's nations and their peoples are at loggerheads as never before, and of the same, the future only promises more.

Clever apps, of human being will make saps.

Innovation and expansion is the corporate world's mission.

Competition is both spurring and deterring.

Professors are serious teachers, not frivolous preachers.

Moderation and compromise spawn welcome surprise.

Not to educate or to train, but to educate and to train.

Of the profound, there are but few around, the dullards, in contrast, ever abound.

Politicians and their half lies are no surprise.

Sleep is a restful retreat for head and for feet.

Leisure is a very rare pleasure.

Things of the mind are as important as things of the body.

To be married need not be to be harried.

Manifest Destiny is manifest conceit.

Prancing is not dancing.

A psychological want can break or make.

Some are both large and small.

The petty are ever fretty.

Feelings lead, thought follows.

Simplicity courts felicity.

Sex will thrill but no less vex.

To compromise is to recognize that we are not alone.

A world that has no weapons, knows no wars.

Individualism is blessing and burden.

Education's focal concern is knowledge and ability, not morality and goodness.

Morality both binds and benefits.

Anarchy is a breath of life that chokes to death.

Humans differ only in their particulars.

Difference is treasured and persecuted.

All ideologies are extremes in their peculiarities.

In its practice, modern capitalism is pure avarice.

Our world has become the corporate world's borderless financial playground.

The Electronic Age will eventually drown in its endless flow of trivia.

One must be strong when all goes wrong.

A sound mind and sound body assure a sound life.

The horns of a dilemma can be sharp.

To write one's thinking is to distill one's thoughts.

The imagination is a treasure trove of unlikely possibilities.

Curiosity and desperation have always sought and found answer and succor in the imagined.

Wars leave victors and vanquished in their wake, but never ever any winners.

Comply or die has become Islam's battle cry.

We eat for the body and fast for the spirit.

To counter the strong, the weak have to be meek.

When choice departs, coercion starts.

Expectation is not obligation.

Struggle energizes and apathy lethargizes.

What can be changed for the better, should be changed.

The conventional beliefs and ways of today become tomorrow's yesterday.

Language is the most effective weapon of both peace and war.

Truths are fiction become belief.

Truths are edifying and facts are pedestrian.

Language can describe, it cannot account for.

We feel too much and think too little.

Truths conflict as much as do falsehoods.

Religions will die but religion will live on.

Nations are dated, confederations are on the horizon.

America's entrepreneurial bubble, like all other bubbles, is sure to burst.

Immigrants have always been a country's proven leaven.

America's plethora of trivial apps promises to become more bane than gain.

Ethics and morality of yore have left America's shore.

Gambling is problem, not solution.

Casinos are costly brothels.

Politics is rewarding game not serious governance.

Don't scratch what does not itch.

Virtue fasts and sin feasts.

Everybody is somebody.

Law punishes, it does not remedy.

Flesh and spirit are at loggerheads.

Hope feeds the spirit while want starves the body.

Rehabilitation is costly, crime is costlier.

The rich tend to be poor in spirit and the poor tend to be rich in spirit.

The possible sates, the impossible fascinates.

Prevention is expensive but cure is more expensive.

Virtue in excess becomes comedy in distress.

Virtue is a flower and sin is a weed.

Philosophy surmises and religion sermonizes.

Life and death are of one, just as are day and night.

For some, little is much, and for others, much is little.

Better to be out of step than to fall in line and keep in step.

The Middle East has become Absurdia politically, and Berserkia socially.

A pact with too many conditions is a pact that will fray for too many reasons.

Prevention is timely action, cure is belated reaction.

An enemy of an enemy is not, ergo, a friend.

Some learn because of, others in spite of, and still others just never learn.

Many eat because they like to eat, some because they have to, and
   still others just eat.

To account for miracles is to discount them.

Most learn too little and forget too much.

To change one's lot for the better, one need only change one's way
   for the better.

Compromise is not a cop-out.

Ever more for some is ever less for others.

Some want much government, others little government, and still
   others couldn't care less for government.

We thrash and flail as best we can, and all too often to little avail.

Too much ready action and too little calm reflection have left the
   whole world in turmoil.

The hopeful Arab Spring has become a long and bitter winter.

Foolish consistency will leave your face without a nose.

Cultural twilight is not a pretty sight.

Apparent rejuvenations are often but actual disintegrations.

What women want, women get.

The quick are not the fast.

One cannot command but that one first know and understand.

To be selective is to be effective.

Cultures begin with a whimper and end with a bang.

Do your best, and then rest.

Cooperation is not a surrender.

To be infatuated is to be incapacitated.

Forethought is better than afterthought, and afterthought is better than no thought.

Communication is the key that opened the door of civilization.

We dislike for too many reasons, and like for too few reasons.

Bodies are tilled and minds lie fallow.

Indulgences have untoward consequences.

Not to protect is to neglect.

Indulgence is foe not friend.

Curiosity kills more rats than cats.

Money makes and breaks the carriage of marriage.

Better to grin and bear it, than to scream and shout.

Don't command, suggest, and don't demand, request.

A stock market is not a charity.

Better to act than to react.

To talk too much is to say too little.

Repetition is not explanation.

Repent before you are spent.

Morality and law are more theory than practice.

Belief, values and way of life drift with the times and their changing winds.

Wall Street is a slick casino, and Main Street is a sick shantytown.

Democracy embraced capitalism, and capitalism effaced democracy.

Music, song and dance cannot but life enhance.

To be skilled or learned is much, to be good is more.

Person is fact, persona is fiction.

Love and hate are of a kind: both are very deaf and blind.

Nothing lasts, nothing is wasted, and nothing is lost.

Mankind's kill at will flouts the Bible's do not kill.

Capitalism of whatever ilk, makes the few and breaks the many.

Morality and law are needed and should be heeded.

If it doesn't pay, it will go away.

More may prove to be less and less may prove to be more.

Advantage and disadvantage travel in tandem.

Health trumps wealth.

When reason and humanity fail, civil turmoil and wars will prevail.

A good conscience promises a good sleep.

Prisons are punishment, not cure.

More education is more growth and more opportunity.

Love is heady and capricious, friendship is steady and tenacious.

Mass education is a grand frustration.

Not education or training, but education and training.

Teaching is a profession, not a job.

Up and walk, when politicians begin their double talk.

The salacious makes and the prudish breaks.

To dare foolishly is to fare accordingly.

Hate if you must or will, but don't fight or kill.

Change is inevitability, not choice.

Heaven or hell above, and peace or war below.

Men shout and curse, women wail and weep.

Better to fraternize than to antagonize.

As we age, banter becomes giggle and bluster becomes gossip.

The healthy are the hearty, the ailing are the wailing.

Thou shalt not kill should be etched on every hill.

At their best, religions are heaven, at their worst, they are hell.

All humans should be valued and nurtured accordingly.

Women are the best agents of good change.

People posture to impress.

Humans are not intrinsically good or bad, they become either or most commonly both.

The world has never been what it could or should be, and never will.

Humans have never been good just to be good.

Look to yourself and not to others.

Prepositions are wild cards.

Just to hope is not to cope.

Doors do not open of their own accord.

To wrought ought calls for thought.

What hasn't been written cannot be read.

Money attracts thieves like monkeys attract fleas.

Much we know but more we don't.

Nothing begins but that it also ends.

Know yourself to better yourself.

Hostility is untoward reaction, not solution.

A smile lights the room, a frown casts a shadow .

Gays, lesbians, transdressers and transgenders are others, but no
less sisters and brothers.

We are actuality and flirt with virtuality.

Given human conduct, hell must want for standing room.

When young, they skip and run, when old, they flay and fold.

Fortune is chance or choice, or both.

One hates most where one loved most.

Regret is hindsight that, in turn, can become foresight.

Trust and good will notwithstanding, pacts are never without
their risks.

When rubber hits road, metal takes off.

Love scorches, hate burns.

Heaven is possible, hell is probable.

When drinkers make the rounds, laughter always abounds.

To be overwrought is to become distraught.

Forethought should prepare the way, and afterthought should
tuck it away.

Hounds run and bay, dogs bark and stay.

It is always the other who engages in terrorism.

Choice is never free of risk.

But for change there'd be no time.

Do your best and to others leave the rest.

To hear is good, to listen is better.

Of itself, space is nothingness.

Listen, then think, read, then reflect.

Time is a measurement, not a reality.

Self-realization trumps wealth accumulation.

To live content is to die content.

To go astray is to be left at bay.

Reason lightens, good will brightens.

Help the helpless and cheer the cheerless.

Change is the mother of time.

To mean well is good, to be mindful's better.

Love it or leave it, is patriotism gone berserk.

Help the needy and chide the greedy.

Thinkers think and doers do, and together the old world
they renew.

Patterns prevail in culture no less than they do in nature.

We do what we do because we are what we are.

Hew to the line or pay a fine.

The daring bare, the rest stay dressed.

Most convictions are but opinions.

To use another is to reduce the self and to abuse a brother.

Normally, men and women neither love nor hate, they just each other tolerate.

Insight and foresight trump hindsight.

Neither conquerors nor vanquished are the better for their wars.

Give where there is want, and help when there is need.

Anger at others is all too frequently but deflected self-anger.

A chronic nervous laugh has nothing to do with humor.

Angry men are powder kegs on legs.

Just to age is not to become a sage.

To flee it, is not to solve it.

Treat your children roughly and they'll respond quite gruffly.

The bitter is no less meet than is the sweet.

Manage anger or anger will manage you.

Joy greets birth, toil and leisure, trouble and pleasure follow, and then dour death its farewell whispers.

There's always a tomorrow to age and blunt our sorrow.

Effort is as important as result.

Better to be slow and meticulous than to be fast and careless.

Remember the past, embrace the present, and prepare for the future.

We learn too little, know even less, and squander too much.

We learn effortfully and forget effortlessly.

Nothing is impossible but the impossible.

Commercial interests are powerful incentives.

Money and material things should not be the sole measure of wealth and poverty.

Independence and initiative take a toll, but also reach a goal.

Better a loner and lonely than to be married and harried.

Starve wants and feed needs.

Try exercise to exorcise your physical pains.

All eat to live, and some live to eat.

Most people are strangers—strangers both to the self and to strangers.

To know about a person is not to know that person.

Love is an exhilarating and blinding attraction that makes and/or breaks its many captives.

Most would if they could, but they can't and don't.

The whole is rarely, if ever, but the sum of its parts.

Work we must, play we should.

Know better, but don't so tell.

To invade is not to aid.

The gods know better, but we are but mortals.

To better know the self is to better know the other.

Depression is a serious affliction, oppression is but an irritation.

Hell is surely more thickly populated than heaven.

Where there's no strife, there's no life.

The circumspect are life's compass, the balanced, its ballast.

Too much action is but activity.

Nervous Nellies have queasy bellies.

Mankind's inhumanity is more abominable than its humanity is
admirable.

We know better after than before.

Believers are assured and thinkers are convinced.

To be chronically angry is to be at odds with both self and others.

To avoid is to ameliorate not to solve.

The poor forage, the wealthy pillage.

Servants oblige, masters compel.

The lazy ones are wily not crazy.

The old lulls to sleep, the new jars awake.

Blue skies and sunshine lure outside, dark clouds and cold wind
keep inside.

To acknowledge and respect another, is to be, and to find a sister
or brother.

A good day's work deserves a good night's rest.

Body and mind not used are abused.

Ideologies that wreak more havoc than do good, are dated and
should be superannuated.

The powerful reveal themselves, the weak conceal themselves.

Men are combative, women know better.

Never is all too often better than ever.

Heaven and hell know no geography.

Winning is too touted and losing is too flouted.

Those who know orate, and those who don't, bloviate.

Some become mellow with growing age, others but add to a
chronic rage.

The oblivious are blind to their oblivion.

Limitations sprout compensation.

The unimpaired see their way, the blind hear and feel their way.

The wealthy give little of their much, the poor give much of
their little.

Flawed we are and err we will.

Weak we are though strong in faith.

The strong are never wrong and the weak just never speak.

Silence born of fear is deadly.

To listen and to see, trumps to hear and to look.

To praise is to raise and to berate is to deflate.

The day breaks and the night falls, but only figuratively.

To disagree peacefully is to agree sensibly.

The wealthy are burdened by their wealth, the poor by their poverty.

To pretend is to offend.

Hear they do, but deaf they are.

Look they do, but see they don't.

We do not live but that we die.

Peace is better possibility, not threat.

Sharp it is, but cut it doesn't.

It is better to reflect than do, than to do then regret.

The sage are prone to listen, fools fill their space with sound.

When virtuality becomes your reality, it's time to visit your friendly psychotherapist.

Children are wide-eyed and bushy-tailed, the old are furrow-browed and tight-lipped.

Better to pause and to settle down than to hurry and be left harried.

Gadgetry has become the digital age's reality.

We bask in the sunshine and take cover in the rain.

Cultural chaos is a dance of death for the few, a lively circus for the many.

Peace is tedious and war is thrilling.

America's democracy, once more or less of the people, by the people and for the people, has become but a means for the monied.

The lazy are not necessarily bad, and the diligent are not necessarily good.

Not to be in and of, is to become a cultural dodo bird.

Women tend to, and men fend off.

We play sub sole and pray sub rosa.

Day and effort enervate, night and rest regenerate.

Life is a many-laned one-way highway.

Humans tend to over-eat and to under-exercise.

Technology and humanism have gone their separate ways.

A world of nations is becoming a world of corporations.

Know yourself to be yourself.

Lies are abhoring but exciting, truths are boring but ennobling.

Better to be spiritually wealthy and materially poverty-stricken than to be materially wealthy and spiritually poverty-stricken.

When words fail, music can prevail.

Love's most at home in music and least of all in thought.

If not quite awake, you're likely to make a mistake.

Taste it, don't waste it.

To vie with others is good, to vie with the self is better.

Moralists are society's necessary nuisances.

Reality is oneness in multiplicity and timelessness in time.

Utter what you will and utter it with will.

Being is cozy, becoming is rosy.

The past is memory and nostalgia, the future is hope and dream, and the present is trial and error.

The other can become a brother.

The possible stirs, the probable whets, and the actual sates.

But for variations, all is as it was, and as it ever will be.

Every culture has its day, then fades away.

Potential is important, application and tenacity are critical.

Genius has its bitter personal price.

All warm-blooded animals are but variations on a theme.

Curiosity stirs, need spurs, and application and tenacity reward.

Goodness has its rewards, but it also takes its toll.

Expediency trumps morality.

The rarer, the more valued.

Foreign lands will go their foreign ways.

Humans are as infallible as they are invisible.

Virtue comes at a price.

Too few humans know enough to know better.

Girls would be cute, and boys look on mute.

To lust is to disgust.

Sounds become meaningful words, and words, meaningfully related, become meaningful language.

People are acculturated and society is accommodated.

Where there is no self-awareness, there is no self.

Thought generates language, and language generates thought.

That man was created after the image of god, is imagination and not explanation.

Any explanation seems better than nary an explanation.

We are wed to a tangible world, and we flirt with a spiritual world.

When hope wanes, desperation gains.

Those who have are in control, and those who have not are controlled.

Preachers and teachers are of a dedicated kind, yet they have always been harder to keep than to find.

The crowd regales, but aloneness prevails.

Unlike earth, heaven knows no financial divide.

Some feel rich, though poor.

To be fearful and wary is to remain alive.

The actively concerned are too few, and the silent observers are too many.

The good old days is what the oldster says.

The good, though poor, have inherited the kingdom of God.

Active involvement is laudable, passive observation is regrettable.

A liberal education transfigures, technological training delivers.

Work is stimulating, indolence is enervating.

The exceptional is less often gift than it is effort.

Rough waters run shallow.

To some much is too little, to others little is too much, and ne'er the twain will meet.

Money has become America's be-all and end-all.

Wealth is more than is needed, and poverty is less than is needed.

Some seem born but to suffer, to moan, and to mourn.

To be pliable is not to break.

Some extend the other cheek, others slap back.

Nature showers to water her flowers.

Men will have their way, and women will have their day.

The poor of means subsist on beans.

To be fearful is to be anxious and tearful.

Women long, men lust.

Obstacles are both impediment and challenge.

Phantasy and play fills a child's every day.

Women want to cradle, men prefer to fondle.

To socialize is to corral and to quell.

The fleet of mind are rarely fleet of feet.

Women lock the door, men break down the door.

To repay in kind will leave too many toothless and blind.

Opinions are common coin, facts are realities, and truths are idealities.

A square wheel holds no appeal.

To be chaste is not a waste.

Banality is an all too common reality.

Morality is a cultural necessity.

We do what we do because we are what we are.

What was impossible yesterday is possible today, and what is impossible today will be possible tomorrow.

When in doubt, instinct is our out.

Animals are tamed, humans are socialized.

The American dream has lost its gleam.

America has lost its way at home and has gone astray abroad.

Don't rage, turn the page.

To know when to retreat, is to avoid defeat.

Better to tell than to compel.

It's best to request, not to demand.

All that becomes, in due time unbecomes.

Today's actual always falls short of tomorrow's possible.

To get ahead is to add and to shed.

Social ladders sport slippery rungs.

Struggle exhilarates and success validates.

A failed effort need one not a failure make.

To do nothing is to be nobody, to do something is to be somebody.

Feed need, starve want.

Too many think what they want to think, and not what they should think.

Most are worse than the worse of their deeds.

Not to challenge the self is to shortchange the self.

All lives matter, and all to the contrary is idle chatter.

Hysteria is the mother of political madness.

Good and evil have since Adam and Eve been locked in never-ending battle.

A roiling world recalls the Bible's Armageddon.

Death is life's horror of horrors.

The good are reflective, the bad are reflexive.

Few come to grips with death, and even fewer to terms.

Not to greet is not meet.

Nothing's up and nothing's down, for everything is always both up and down.

It's not meet to bleat in defeat.

Wealth enables and poverty disables.

Morality persuades, expediency compels.

Hosts should be gracious and guests should be grateful.

When that shadowy figure with scythe at the threshold stands, put aside all immediate plans.

It's easy to be naughty, a challenge to behave.

We grumble as we look back with regret and look forward with hope.

Be indolent if you will, but don't pretend fatigue.

Minds misused are minds abused.

A sound body with a sound mind is a rare find.

Skill alone does not art make.

Humans are alive primarily to live and to procreate.

Art is in the mind of the beholder.

Where there's life, there's self-assertion.

Life feeds on life.

In our aging western Judeo-Christian culture, a tired humanism has faded away and an energetic technology now holds sway.

The Bible's dos and don'ts are no less flouted than they are touted.

To defer is to be polite, and to demur is to slight.

Help the needy to help themselves.

Words prepare the way, deeds are the way.

Invasive plants need little care, but they'll soon get into your hair.

Fools count their shekels, the wise count their blessings.

Be furious if you must but don't become malicious.

Money of itself is a very poor measure of real wealth.

The righteous are right and the self-righteous are wrong.

Our true young are the young in spirit.

Be hysterical if you will, but don't become physical.

The strong are never wrong and the weak are never right.

Good health is true wealth.

One reaps as one sows, but only in the absence of crows.

Stand upright and be forthright.

Take things in hand, don't let them get out of hand.

Mankind is no less destructive than it is constructive.

Be foolish but don't become a fool.

Words and deeds gauge the self.

Growth economy will bubble and burst.

The holier-than-thou never cease to vow.

The conductor has his head and baton, the herdsman, his voice and whip.

Humans are as creative in their destructiveness as they are in their constructiveness.

All others are potential brothers.

Hate does not elevate.

Moderation has never been in good supply, and common sense has ever gone awry.

Discontent will leave one rent.

Neither love nor hate will ever abate.

A busybody is not a workaholic.

Teachers learn to teach, then teach and learn.

One learns to learn, while learning.

School is never out, as long as we're about.

Church bells toll our arrival, and church bells toll our departure.

The able do and the impaired are spared.

Whence, whither, why? Answers they defy.

The heedless are headless.

The rational self is servant to the emotional self.

To become you, feel, think and do.

Each is a walking novel.

To know our whence and whither, and their why, is to know the unknowable.

For the world's wealthy, death is paradise lost, for the world's poor, death is paradise found.

Absolute freedom is absolute nonsense.

Mankind's imperfections fuel its passion for perfection.

Fits of temper should remain tempests in a teapot.

Soughing wind and creaking boughs both stir and soothe.

The old need not be worn or stale.

Of the slow, some are slackers and some are scarred.

Two nickels still make a dime.

To kill another is to kill one's own humanity.

Honest effort is its own reward.

Thinkers don't kowtow, they shake and remake.

The similar prefer the similar.

The amiable and pert tend to flirt

Opposites attract but don't interact.

People of a kind soon find themselves and bind.

But for mountains, there'd be no valleys.

Oh to be healthy, wealthy and wise.

To live mindfully is to live healthfully.

When things go wrong, stand strong, and when things go right, continue the good fight.

Think rapidly and reflect slowly.

An itchy mind deserves a scratch.

An epigram a day will keep boredom at bay.

Hunters and hunted are flipsides of a coin.

Consumerism is impoverishing the many and enriching the few.

To know better should persuade one to do better.

Things are important, humans are more important.

Growth economy is roller coaster economy.

Black slavery never ended, it has only evolved.

Humanity has flown the coop, and inhumanity rules the roost.

The world is out of joint. Oh cursed spite that Hamlet's not here to set it right.

No day, good or bad, is here to stay.

As all goes, so go your woes.

What is authority but legalized power?

Don't shirk or crawl, stand up and stand tall.

Indeed, help where there is distress and need.

Do what the Good Book would have.

If loose of tongue, be fleet of feet.

Genius and insanity commonly walk hand in hand.

The young are anything but timid, and the old are anything but bold.

To be driven can drive to madness.

Life's demands of today leave too many riven and bend, driven and spent.

Humans create their hell and long for heaven.

What we see and what we hear, triggers and determines what we feel and what we think.

Every change demands yet another change.

Every life has its trail of death.

The knots we tie are unravelled by time.

Love stems the tide of death.

Women cherish companionship, men prefer dalliances.

Too many come and go and leave no trace behind.

Change knows no rest, and change never tires.

Informed opinion deserves informed response.

Truths and beliefs, though arguably relative, benefit society and individual immeasurably.

Passion and practicality are ever at variance.

Devices and apps change lives, but do they enrich life?

To add is easy, to edit is difficult.

Our Golden Age of Technology is proving to be too much ado about too little.

To make friends of foes will reduce one's woes.

Papal Infallibility is a quaint antiquity.

Too much of the Electronic Age's glitter is not gold.

Royalty was once earth's divinity.

Life should be embraced and not just suffered.

The novel energizes, the familiar lethargizes.

Novels are imagined , life is lived.

Physical connection without emotional connection is short-term connection.

Technology's adolescent geniuses have yet to learn that all that glitters is not gold.

History is much more than politics and war.

Change itself is an agent of change.

To pretend is to offend.

Suspicion can save one's skin.

The disparity in wealth between the world's few and its many has become a bitter hilarity.

Feel need and starve greed.

The weak can be unctuous, the strong, rambunctious.

Society's predators have become its pillars.

The strong can't do wrong and the weak have to be meek.

The modest hide their light under a bushel, the brash put theirs on display.

The greedy are rarely the needy.

Appreciate what is and let be what is not.

Inactivity has consequences no less than does activity.

Tomorrows and yesterdays are as important as our todays.

Life's pluses should be thankfully embraced and the minuses fully accepted.

Each self goes its own unpredictable way and in its own unpredictable way.

Power does what power is.

Human beings are human animals.

Life is but a chance dance, without purpose and without meaning.

Some humans are more human than animal, and some humans are more animal than human.

To prevent is better than to cure.

Better to reap the benefit than to pay the penalty.

It's not the product, it's the marketing.

Dead fish don't swim upstream.

People become like their world and the world becomes like its people.

Everything has its consequences.

There is much that each can do, and more that each cannot do.

The military does not educate, it trains.

When you do what you do, you get what you get.

Want what you need and not what you want.

Expectation enjoys elation and suffers frustration.

A fool's a fool whether young or old.

Square wheels are good brakes.

No person is this or that, but this and that and much else.

Thy will be done is belief and relief.

Enchantments of whatever ilk are here to come and go and not
to stay.

Goodness is not a commercial commodity.

It is good to be bright, better to be good, and best to be both
bright and good.

That one can hear and see is proof of one's reality.

Passion coupled with compassion is a good antidote for what ails
a country politically and economically.

Not to know oneself is to be without ballast and compass.

To remain is to cling and to hope, to go is to dare and grope.

Sprightly youth looks to the future and weary age looks to the past.

To bloviate is to exasperate and not to explicate.

When things go awry, some cry, others lie.

The discreet do what is meet.

We begin small, wrinkled and pale, and end, tall, bent and frail.

Thinkers think too little and feelers feel too much.

The thin are ever forth and back, the fat prefer to sit and snack.

Children are streams and adults are ponds.

Teaching is a profession, but too few teachers are professionals.

Some push and pull, others are pushed and pulled.

Unbridled capitalism gives to the few and takes from the many.

Choice can make or break.

To have less is not to be less.

Some sing and dance, others sit and grumble.

Look to the self before you turn to another.

It begins with the self and ends with the self.

Choose wisely or pay dearly.

To know more is not to be more.

Life is an endless lesson.

Better that consequences and not inclination determine choice.

Some suffer life and lament, others embrace and love it, and all
    for too little reason.

Human beings might more accurately be termed human animals.

Tranquility, thy name is futility.

Refugees flee, immigrants seek.

The technologists are in, the humanists are out, and the world of
    culture is anything but better for the rout.

Globalization is rapidly ending the era of nations.

The old get wiser, the young but older.

To have aught is to be somebody, to have naught is to be nobody.

To reduce another is not to raise the self.

Would-be's are are-not's.

Trust is reflective, distrust is reflexive.

To kill and eat is to live and thrive.

Aloneness is a physical fact, loneliness is a psychological experience.

The fast make off, the slow are picked off.

The spirit-flesh dichotomy has never ceased to be an agony.

Earth is a splendid mystery to be admired and not a problem to be solved.

Curiosity bestirs, compulsiveness compels.

Mankind's best and worst is born of its innate curiosity and compulsiveness.

A measure of leisure is truly a pleasure.

To get to the bottom of it, you've got to be on top of it.

A dog does not bite the hand that feeds it.

New tastes tease and old tastes please.

The new is a thrill, the old was a thrill.

The foreign ruffles and the familiar calms.

Savor the new exotic flavor, then back to the old familiar fare.

Good will smiles, ill will frowns.

Competition brings out the worst and the best, and in that order.

Some are more body-minded, while others are more spirit-concerned.

Forest fires can rejuvenate or decimate.

Mind over matter is more than verbal patter.

Sing in Spring and bawl in Fall.

Twilight rounds sharp edges, softens harsh glare, and mellows all sounds.

When all else fails, mercy prevails.

Forgive and forget, and don't regret.

To reflect upon the past and the present is always a good beginning for tomorrow.

The business of war is not the business of the people.

Epigrams, apothegms and aphorisms are brief and pithy truisms.

Until there are no others, humans will no be sisters and brothers.

Wars have become a popular and profitable political pastime.

You can afford more if you spend less.

Some ever profess that more can be done by less.

Short skirts attract flirts.

Tattlers are both loathed and lofted.

Faith converts while power subverts.

Actors are their roles.

The female is life's queen, the male is but her consort.

Every individual is a unique ever-changing but essentially never-changing self.

Moderation is a cheap panacea.

Hope burns eternal, but only if stoked.

War rends, peace mends, and this never ends.

Hearts can be softened, minds are hardened.

Male sexuality and aggression walk hand in hand.

The self is chance and choice.

You do what you do because you are what you are.

To understand fully is to pardon fully.

Love is life's binding bond.

Trivial imponderables should be laid to rest, and the sooner the better.

To be worthwhile, life must have its smile.

Love generates energy and hate expends it.

Feel and think before you act.

Some become wizened, others become wise, and still others become both wizened and wise.

Life is roil and toil for the many, and dance and romance for the few.

The embraced of today is the rejected of tomorrow.

Where there is water, there is life.

All God's creatures, both big and small, are both independent and interdependent.

We cannot but play the cards we are dealt.

Forgive and forget, lest you regret.

Heed and help, where want is felt.

To blindly trust and believe is to be very naive

To persist is to prevail, to desist is to fail.

Surmise is less judgment than it is surprise.

Earth is imperfect and Heaven is less than perfect.

To sow insults is to harvest insults.

Aloneness is fate and loneliness is chance.

The male uses the female for his purposes and the female uses the male for her purposes.

Wealth and power is ever more desirous of more wealth and power.

If you hear something, say something.

Mass imprisonment for too little reason poses more problem than it solves.

More freedom and less oppression would spawn a new and better world.

Problems are opportunities for solutions.

As of yore, preachers exhort, and teachers implore.

The present is born of the past and foreshadows the future.

Ever bigger, ever faster, ever better and ever more, has become the myopic credo that motivates the corporate world.

Possessions of themselves do not a better individual make.

When things become obsessions, humans themselves become things.

The righteous will inherit the Kingdom of God, and sinners will live riotously in hell.

The different are treated differently.

Humanism answered, technology delivers.

Contentment is a hope, happiness is a dream.

National exceptionalism is rare chutzpah.

Humanism had its day, now technology holds sway.

Work is both a pain and a gain.

Happiness is but happenstance.

Expectations can breed frustrations.

Diligence is more profit- than virtue-minded.

Impatience makes for revolution, patience allows for evolution.

Nostalgia is a sad remembrance of things past.

Human beings are not good or bad, they are both good and bad.

Revolution upsets and evolution resets.

Our world of nations is rapidly becoming a world of corporations.

Pain is not without its gain.

Social changes begin with individual changes.

Absolute freedom is absolute disaster.

Physically, the human condition has certainly changed for the better but metaphysically, it has no less certainly remained the perplexing mystery it has always been.

Habit and reward fashion lives.

Harness technology or be harnessed by it.

Lives are shaped by instant gratification

Empathy is a bridge that links, apathy is a gulf that separates.

Some are most alive when filled by hatred and engaged in battle.

History has always been part fact and part fiction.

Wisdom is a distillate of experience, knowledge and good judgment.

To admit error is strength, not weakness.

Losing can smart, and can also make smarter.

Few are those who are not both victors and victims.

One can be small, though tall.

Most live in the now and here, fewer in the then and there.

Where there's no water, there's no life.

To be used is to be abused.

We are what those are with whom we choose to be.

Like feelings, thoughts are both bliss and agony.

One cannot be what one is not.

Epigrams epitomize.

Humans are as incomprehensible as the weather is unpredictable.

No one is spared the wear and tear of time and care.

About me, without me, is an invasion of privacy.

Capitalism knows no decency and feels no shame.

The sexes use and abuse each other, much to their joy and much to their grief.

Better to extend a hand than to clench a fist.

Radical individualism's "go your way and do your thing," is more brawn than brain.

Envy is a futile frenzy.

Hate and love are as irrational as they are intensive.

Women tend to be fussy and men are messy.

To heed and to feed is a good deed.

Mutual appreciation and respect is to mutual advantage.

Life makes some and breaks others.

Justice delayed is justice denied.

To be is good sense, to seem is pretence.

Not to reveal is to conceal.

Just to tread water is not to swim.

Truth has taken wing and the internet has become a beehive
    of lies.

Eyes are closed to see what was and what will be.

Children are visible and vocal.

Mortals would be Gods, and Gods are but mortals.

To say it's so, does not make it so.

Restless mankind has left a glorious mess in its turbulent wake.

Hope for the good and accept the bad.

An epigram a day, the blues will allay.

Of public education, too much is but indoctrination.

Every change both betters and worsens.

Thinking begets thinking.

The first hired, the last fired.

Memory is ballast and hope is compass.

Twin peaks adorn the female façade.

To cherry-pick one's way through life if but to die not having lived.

But for fear, most would not be here.

But few come both to grips and to terms with life.

Fear is a protective buffer, without which life would be much rougher.

Physically and psychologically, with the passing years, children become more and more what their parents are.

Explanation is clarification, exhortation is obfuscation.

From those who have should be taken, and to those who have not should be given.

To regulate is not to appropriate, but just to keep in line.

Consolidation is a boon for the corporate world, a bane for the working world.

A boon for the few is a bane for the many.

Day enervates, night generates.

Music is mankind's balm of balms.

Much that is new is but a variant of the old.

Lies have always trumped truth.

Violence is almost always reflexive response.

Hatred is deep-seated and long-winded.

Religion is morality's enforcing handmaiden.

Earth is justice gone awry, heaven a justice fulfilled.

Prolonged reflection can be calculated deflection.

Smiles are an upper, frowns are a downer.

One must oft go backward to go forward.

Electronic devices may be smart, humans are smarter.

Freedom without economic security is a pipe dream.

Health care is a right, not a privilege.

To stroll at night, is to dress in white.

Nota bene, measure twice before you cut.

Every human being is an unicum, and every life is unique.

Nomads are at home wherever they choose to roam.

It is all too human to reflect too little, to lie too readily, to react too reflexively, and to believe too blindly.

Kill or be killed is a battle cry, not a peace plea.

The Electronics Age is anything but sage.

The myriad novelties of the digital age will have their day, in time will cloy, and then will fade away.

Religion and politics have always been agents of both peace and war, and this is likely ever to be the case.

To stroll at dark, is no safe lark.

Smart electronic devices are more novelty than necessity.

Extraordinary circumstances demand extraordinary measures.

Our world is peopled by too many nobodies disguised as somebodies.

Appearance attracts, distracts and repels, and does so more wrongly than rightly.

We want what we've not had.

To hear and to heed is to acknowledge need.

Silence can be loud.

Some glean and others just preen.

Noone is a nobody.

Not to have ought is to be nought.

Ultimately culture will fail, and nature will prevail.

Today's hope for a better world is draped in black.

Hope is more possibility than it is probability.

Romance is fickle chance.

A little charm will do no harm.

Better to know than to but guess.

Military solutions leave problems in their wake.

But for ears, there'd be no sound.

When companies merge, profits surge.

Gifts can demand more than they afford.

Heeded pain ends in gain.

Better to befriend than to belittle.

A chance dance can lead to romance.

It is no fun to be on the run.

We thirst and hunger though quenched and sated.

Slow wits are easy hits.

Self-deprecation is palliative, not cure.

Anger is but brief satisfaction.

Just because you can, doesn't mean you should.

Mass shopping is mass therapy.

All are given to thought, but few are thinkers.

Men are destructive, women are seductive.

Substance is persuasive, appearance is illusive.

To dismiss God is to invite the devil.

Success intoxicates, setback sobers.

That was then and this is now. Period!

Peace and war are life's wedded givens.

When its religion is spent, society is left rent.

Otherness should be befriended and not belittled.

Racial difference is not racial inferiority.

The poor and humble, weak, meek and helpless, are life's flotsam and jetsam.

The poor are troubled by their poverty, the rich are burdened by their wealth.

The path of morality is challenging, the road of immorality is inviting.

To deviate from the conventional is to be deemed asocial.

Heaven is a theocracy, earth is a slopocracy.

The ideal is as elusive as it is attractive.

Too many are too much of our too troubled world.

Estrangement and not intimacy, is the fruit of today's much espoused electronic mode of communication.

"Upgrade" has become the buyer's song and dance, and the corporate world smiles all the way to the bank.

Difference is not good cause for belligerence.

We are interconnected with many, but know few if any.

We should think before we speak, while we speak, and after we speak.

To know oneself is to better know the other.

To foul-mouth is to expel foul breath.

The pearly gates are portals to erewhon.

One person's attractions are another's distractions.

The present is born of the past and the future is born of the present and the past.

Wars should be terminated, not propagated.

Heaven is but earth etherealized.

The shopping mall is a foretaste of heaven's plentitude.

A good epigram a day should your doldrums surely allay.

The present-minded opt for "more now, less later," and the future-minded opt for "less now, more later."

To behave is to oblige others, to misbehave is to indulge the self.

For many, all is tunnel, for few, all is light.

Today's attractions are tomorrow's distractions.

Better to do and to regret than never to have done.

To do is to stew, and not to do is to rue.

Vowels sing, consonants sputter.

Success is inflative and failure is deflative.

To weep is a relief, not a cure.

Sympathy and empathy are the hallmarks of humanity.

Money and sex lure and hex.

Sex is a raw appetite, love is an intimate relationship.

Christmas gifting has become onerous obligation and rank expectation.

To relent and repent is to be left content.

One may give up without giving in.

Summer lavishes and winter ravages.

To make war is to savage and to ravage.

Stasis lulls and dulls, change agitates and stimulates.

Romantic love is "you and I," sexual love is "I and you."

Theocracies can be benign, and democracies can be devastating.

America is wealthy, thanks to its poverty.

Too many humans are but bumps on a rolling log.

Thinking solves old problems only to generate new problems.

Too much of anything can be devastating.

POEMS

Poets give and readers complement.

The Now

There is no yesterday,
There is no tomorrow.
There is no past,
There is no future.

There is no future
On the horizon.
There is no past
In today's wake.

These are but concepts
Not realities.
There's but a Now,
A fleeting Now!

Such it is!

As I do age,
Now frail and weak,
Quite stiff in body
And soft of mind,
My thoughts oft dwell
On a dear past,
Lament the present,
And fear the coming!

There's nothing new
In this old stew:
A well-worn path
All oldsters tread
Before the end
And faint adieu.

Such it is,
Has always been!

It all depends...

There is no in
And there's no out,
For what is in
Is also out.

There is no above
And there's no below,
For what's above
Is also below.

There is no up
And there's no down,
For what is up
Is also down.

There is no big
And there's no small.
For what is big
Is also small.

There is no good
And there's no bad,
For what is good
Is also bad.

It all depends
On context,
Relationship,
Comparison.

Contrary to the Core

We love and are loved,
We nurture and are nurtured,
We praise and are praised,
We protect and are protected,
We heal and are healed,
We help and are helped,
We give and are given,
We placate and are placated,
We encourage and are encouraged,
We appreciate and are appreciated.

We hate and are hated,
We abuse and are abused,
We denigrate and are denigrated,
We use and are used,
We hurt and are hurt,
We take and are taken,
We cheat and are cheated,
We berate and are berated,
We deceive and are deceived,
We betray and are betrayed.

It's not either or,
It's a mix of both.
We do what we should do,
And also what we shouldn't.
A mess we've always been,
Contrary to the core.
That's life in its essence.
We can not but try
To nurse the positive
And curb the negative.

Two Peas of a Pod

Israelis and Palestinians were for each other made,
Each has abetted the other's wanton purposes,
Each persists though all has gone from bad to worse,
And nothing's been learned nor is anything likely to be learned.

Israelis found their scapegoat in the Palestinians,
Palestinians found their scapegoat in the Israelis.

Palestinians are a butt for the ire of the Israelis,
Israelis are a butt for their ire of the Palestinians.

Both camps are clearly both victim and obdurate perpetrator,
And each is rent by moral and political indignation.

Both camps are obviously right and just as clearly wrong,
And neither is about to recognize the truth!

Though culturally, politically and economically worlds apart,
Both camps are in their endless feud but two peas of a pod.
Neither party is apt to relent and to change its ways.
The writing on the wall is clear, but remains unheeded.

Seaward swarming lemmings rush their fatal way!

Ein ewiger Augenblick

Die Sonne geht unter,
Im Zwielicht ein Märchenland:
Verwandelt die Welt,
Kein Lärm, kein Streit, kein Kampf,
Alles im leichten Dunst
Stille und zaubernd beleuchetet,
Kein gestern, kein morgen,
Ein ewiger Augenblick!

Better Possibility

Every truth falls short of truth
And all views in part are biased.
This we know but little heed.

Truth and views have always been
Mankind's guiding absolutes,
The cause of endless human turmoil.

If humans are to become more civil,
And nations less belligerent,
We need but pause and change our ways.

We need only take to heart
That every truth falls short of truth,
That all views in part are biased,
Then say and do accordingly.

The Old and the New

The threadbare Judeo-Christian garb
Of our Western World is rapidly tattering.
A culture has almost run its course,
And a void of chaos will soon follow.

Cultured voids spawn cultural novelty:
Seeds of new thought germinate,
Yarn for tomorrow's cultural cloak
May already be on the spinning wheel.

Cultures come and cultures go,
Each has its day, then fades away!
Ours it is to mourn the old
And to hail the budding new.

Bewildered

I'm old
And am spent.
I'm anxious
And am rent.
I fear
The end is near.

Whatever was,
Is memory.
What is,
Is foreign.
And tomorrow
Is void of promise.

Still in,
But not of.
Adrift
In the wake of change,
An alien
In what was home.

Alive too long,
Too fixed to change,
Too given to loss,
Too blind to gain,
Too stunned to think,
Encased in gloom.

Bewildered I wait
For the sun to set!

Our Ken

We can measure
And can describe.
We categorize
And analyze.
But all else
A mystery remains.

Why all is
And is as it is,
And why all changes
As it ever does,
Is quite beyond
All human ken.

Things there are
We cannot do,
And things there are
We cannot think.
We are but mortals,
And gods we're not.

Vain Questions

Whence, whither, why?
The mysteries of life!
We'll never cease to ask
And we'll never know.

As We Age

Age is a progressive transformation,
A challenge for both body and mind.

All that we once were is gone:
We toil more slowly and tire more quickly;
We eat more slowly and are sated more quickly;
We injure more easily and heal less readily;
We doze more frequently and sleep more fitfully;
We think more laboriously and reminisce more reflexively;
We anger more readily and forgive more begrudgingly;
We take umbrage more often and become depressed more easily;
We are less engaged and become more fidgety;
We are more fearful and become less tolerant;
We are more estranged by change and become more lonely.

Aging ends in helpless impotence,
As pending death its ominous shadow casts!

Woes

Some bear their woes in silence,
Become confused and limp,
Just groan and moan in private.

And though most their grief in silence bear,
A chosen few, like Goethe and his Tasso,
Have broken rank to speak their inner plight.

Like Goethe, troubled Tasso found his voice:
"Und wenn der Mensch in seiner Qual verstummt
Gab mir ein Gott zu sagen, wie ich leide."

In English and poetry rendered, this would read:
And whilst most humans suffer silently,
God granted me the voicing of my woes.

Beyond all Ken

Cosmic night,
Gaseous roil,
Matter then,
Inert mass
Without shape,
Timeless time.

Spheres then shaped,
Among them earth
Spinning round a sun
And whirling ever.
Seasons followed
And night the day.

A miracle followed,
The birth of life
From mere matter.
A second wonder,
Self-awareness,
Conscious life.

From gas masses
To inert matter,
To beings alive,
Self-consciousness,
Thinking humans.
A wondrous path
Beyond all ken!

An Aside

Hear and heed,
Look and see,
Think and do,
And night will follow
As surely the day.
Thou willst not then
Shortchange yourself.

Life's Flow

What I once was,
I am no more:

The blush of youth,
The swells of vigor,
The rushes of hope,
The facile mind,
The ready smiles,
The spur of dreams,
The joys of love,
The charge of feats,
The lures of life,
The happy flight
Of endless time,
All has become
But memory,
Recall of was,
Of vibrant youth.

Remember do,
Nought's here to stay.
It's time to mourn
But not lament.

Some and Others

Some are given to the here, others to the beyond,
Some to the present, others to the past,
Some to the body, others to the soul.

Some are very social, others very reclusive,
Some are humble, others arrogant,
Some are giving, others taking.

Some opt for thought, others for feelings,
Some for knowledge, others for ignorance,
Some for diligence, others for indolence.

Some are passive, others aggressive,
Some are empathic, others indifferent,
Some are timid, others daring.

We are the some, and we are the others,
And we all share in these traits and all others.
Each may remain what each may be,
And each may change should each so choose.
The choice is yours and the choice is mine,
As too are the rewards of whatever kind.

Let Be

Let live what can and wills to live,
Let die the tired and spent.

Each creature has its span of time
In tune with nature's way.

Let be what is and what was meant to be,
And let life take its lotted course, no less!

Either Or

Fight or flight,
Persuasion or evasion.

The former's natural,
The latter's cultural.

The former's reflexive,
The latter's reflective.

The former's for the many,
The latter's for the few.

But that mankind evolve for the better,
Such life has been, is and will be!

Basic Questions

Who are we?
Whence, whither and why?
We philosophize,
We hypothesize,
But all's in vain,
Beyond our ken,
And that's good.

There are things
We'll never know,
And shouldn't know.
All unveiled
Would quickly sate,
Would leave us bare
And in despair.

Man's a mystery,
Life's a mystery.
Let both be
What both are!

Such It Is

For some, life is
A hell of toil and tears.
For others, life is
A vale of love and joy.

I've known hell and vale,
Suffered and rejoiced,
Am the better for it,
And know but gratitude.

The Ebb of Time

As sunset pales and shadows grow,
And as din fades and silence spreads,
My feelings fly and all thoughts falter,
My eyelids weary and slumber beckons.

Day's nigh spent and life's in ebb,
But all's not over, not yet done,
My sands of time, though swirling fast,
Have yet to leave my hourglass bare.

Though weary in body, I'm still active,
Though frayed in emotions, I still feel,
And my mind's still in command.
For that, my smile of gratitude!

Our Few

Some think— the introverted,
Others do— the extroverted,
And still others both think and do.
These are our few, our balanced models,
Those whom we ought to emulate,
Society would be the better for it.

Time and Change

Time does not flow!
It does not come
And it does not go.
Change is perceived
And time is conceived.
Time is a concept,
And change, a reality!

A Madness

Society's structure is in a whirl of change,
Its pace of life is far too fast and harried.
But few can cope with this hectic change and speed
And ever more are falling by the wayside.
How much longer before this madness falters?

A Rush of Change

I who once was in life's vanguard,
Now find myself in a choppy wake.
I who once was in control,
Am now floundering quite bewildered.

Life today's in frenzied flux.
An old world in lumbering flow
And a familiar way of life,
Were swept away by a tsunami,
A tidal wave of drastic change.
An exuberant Electronics Age.

Our yesterworld of industries,
Of toil and tears and aging credos,
Has by and large been thrust aside,
Flooded by wondrous devices and apps,

Become a stimulant institutionally
And a keen diversion socially,
Leaving all things cultural
To slowly wither on the vine.

Cultures come and cultures go,
Our humanistic world of yore
Does but exemplify this flow.
The Electronics Age has emerged full blown,
A world of exciting novelties,
Of ingenious gadgetry,
Of once undreamed of possibility,
A heaven on earth for its committed.

To many of yesteryear's still living,
This technological world of electronics
Is anything but a Golden Age:
A once reflective human culture
Is now a wasteland of digital toys,
An adolescent culture of things,
Of apps and games, videos and tablets,
And of smart phones ad nauseam,
All here and gone ere comprehended,
For youth a ball, for age a pain.

This digitalized and coporatized world of ours,
Little concerned, and with no time
For such once treasured cultural interests
As things philosophical, psychological and literary,
Has left such on-in-years as me,
Chagrined, disillusioned and estranged.

I'm still in, but of, I'm not,
A stranger in what was once my home,
A disgruntled but peaceful Luddite
Resigned to change's inevitabilities!

Dawn and Eve

Dawn slowly asserts itself,
A misty world emerges.
Life blinks and stirs anew,
Then, given to light, we toil.
Crescendo

The twilight shadows grow,
The din of day retreats.
All toil gives way to thought,
Then, wrapped in night we sleep.
Descrescendo

Age and Loss

I'm troubled by my obvious aging,
By my physical deterioration
And by the flagging of my mind.
Of what avail my sensitivities?
A common existential lot,
And acceptance is beyond me.

I mourn my loss of the familiar,
Of old haunts and of old friends,
The painful flow of rapid change.
I mourn the passing of old ways,
Of old beliefs and of old values,
All more treasured for their loss.

The growing pall of age and loss,
Has left me tried and wallowing in woe,
Buoyed by but a spark of cheer.
It could be different but rarely is.
Calm acceptance of the inevitable
Is beyond the reach of most.

C'est la vie!

We

We come and we go,
Whence, whither, why
We'll never know.

We are, to be sure,
But what we think we are
Is only surmise.

We know that we come and we go,
But what, whence, whither, why
Will remain beyond our reach.

The Concept Space

Space is not here or there,
Space is really nowhere
And even everywhere.
It is also nothing
And no less a something.

Like time, its kindred thought,
Space is beyond our senses,
And but for heavenly bodies
And sundry separate things,
There'd be no trace of space.

What separates all objects,
Spawns the notion space,
Just as change births time,
Indeed, time and space are one:
Concepts both, while things and change are realities!

Oneness and Timelessness

Earth's general flux is a clear reality,
As too is the ever change of every life.
Time too is clearly evidenced to all
In this prevailing flux of changing things.
But is all just this and nothing more?
Need all be but what it seems to be?

All depends upon one's view of things.
Upon one's outer and one's inner eye.
The actual eye perceives a flow of changes,
The mental eye erases all time spaces,
Featuring the reality of a life in all its oneness
And the timelessness behind all time.

The outer eye, in all its limitations,
Sees the actual but in its many stages
And is acutely aware of passing time.
The inner eye, in all its mystical ways,
Makes oneness of all multiplicity
And blots out sense of time for timelessness.

It all depends upon one's review of things.
We live in a trying world of change and time,
But can also, in a mystical mental way,
Transcend our old fragmented actuality
And find a tranquil oneness in perpetual change,
And a restful timelessness in restive time.

At any one moment, each living being is all
He or she ever was, is, and ever will be:
A magical oneness in multiplicity
In a magical timelessness of time.

Dismal Days

To be alone,
And to feel forsaken;
To be modest,
And to fumble gauchely;
To dream and hope,
And to try and fail;

To feel inadequate,
And to have no self-esteem;
To be sensitive,
And to suffer endless slight;
To be pressed for time,
And to be left a nervous wreck;

To be a loner of one's choice,
And to be distraught and feel rejected;
To be willing and able too,
And to be dismissed a mediocrity;
To be mindful of self and others,
And to feel apart and quite estranged.

Such have been my many dismal spells,
Days that pained and left me quite distressed.
But such bleak moments only spurred me on
To a renewal of effort and new success,
To periods of satisfaction and contentment
That more than balanced my bleak and dreary days.

Religion and the Self

Christianity is intent upon a perfection of the self.
Buddhism upon the extinction of the self.
Confucianism opts for a better social self.
And Taoism for the tranquil self.

It All Depends

Nothing's up and nothing's down
For what's up is also down.
Nothing's in and nothing's out,
For what's in is also out.

Nothing's short and nothing's long,
For what's short is also long.
Nothing's near and nothing's far,
For what's near is also far,

Nothing's slow and nothing's fast,
For what's slow is also fast.
Nothing's soft and nothing's hard,
For what's soft is also hard.

Nothing's good and nothing's bad,
For what's good is also bad.
Nothing's right and nothing's wrong,
For what's right is also wrong.

All's relative,
All's but view,
And that's not new!

The Lame and the Sound

It is the lame who really walk,
The tongue-tied who really talk,
Said the poet to the nodding philosopher.

It is the sound of body who walk,
The facile of tongue who talk,
Said the philistine to the nodding athlete.

Balanced Change

When it comes to change,
To change of whatsoever ilk,
Some can and others can't,
Some will and others won't.

The pliant will oblige
And the rigid resist.
The result is compromise,
Change in moderation.

No one is right pleased
And no one real distressed.
Difference makes a difference,
And progress evolves more balanced!

Never Stop

If one is to keep on growing,
If one is to know oneself,
One must never cease to test
The limits of one's limited self.

Mind and body must keep evolving,
Horizons must keep on receding,
If one is to keep on growing,
If one is to know oneself,
And if one is to make a difference!

Metaphorically Speaking

When it rains, women get wetter than men.
When it snows, blacks get colder than whites.
When it hails, gays get more pelted than straights.
Social, not existential inequities!

Guess!

Religion was once our source of truth,
Science is that well today.
What does tomorrow hold in store?
Guess we can, but nothing more!

In Nuce

Love affairs are poetry,
Relationships are short story,
And marriages are novels!

Wisdom

To think and then to act,
To act and then to think,
Is wisdom in a nutshell.

The Barbarism of Today

Look around at America socially and politically.
Where is the outrage against our barbarism?
Look around at the world socially and politically.
Where is the outrage against its barbarism?
Where the outrage that finds its expression in action?

Like children, we are all too preoccupied with our toys:
Our philosophers are too preoccupied with intangibles,
Our lay thinkers too preoccupied with thought,
Our scientists too preoccupied with knowing,
Our electronic technicians too preoccupied with gadgetry,
And the common man is too preoccupied with trivia.

Both the few and the many have settled for laissez-faire,
And the lone stray outcries go unheeded!

Free Will

One wills what one wills
Because one is what one is.
So much for free Will!

Extravagance

Americans buy too extravagantly,
Use too briefly and discard too readily.
Of the waste, too little is reclaimed,
Too much despoils both land and water.

To acquire less and to appreciate longer
Must become a new way of life,
And to recycle ever more
Is choice no longer, but necessity.

The Dance of Life

The thinking self is intent upon knowing,
And is anxious to avoid ignorance.
The emotional self is intent upon pleasure,
And is anxious to avoid pain.
The moral self is intent upon the right,
And is anxious to avoid the wrong.
The religious self is intent upon belief,
And is anxious to avoid hell.

To aspire to and to recoil from
Are the very dance of life!

Hate's Many Faces and Dire Way

Human beings traffic in hatred.
The other, the stranger, the outsider
Is suspect, troubling and feared,
And what is feared is quickly hated.

Other appearance and other behavior
Alert, alarm and put on guard,
And slight or affront, real or imagined,
Is enough for anger to turn to hate.
Black and white, yellow and brown
All go this interactive path.

This common personal path to hatred
Has its institutional level:
Nations in their otherness
Have always shared distrust and anger,
And anger has ever peaked in hate.
The otherness of our religions
Has, like that of our many nations,
Ever spawned its share of hate.
What's true of nations and religions
Is no less true of our varied races.
Otherness has ever birthed its hate.
Though less abrasive than that of face,
Ethnicity's otherness has always
Irked and spread its share of hate.

The other, the alien, is rarely a brother.
We commonly hate and are commonly hated,
And the road from hate to violence
Is both well-travelled and very short.

Hate is our order of the day,
And hate is likely here to stay:
A beast that cannot be kept at bay,
An old nemesis that won't go away

Hate's many faces and dire way
Are our human condition on full display.

EPIGRAMS

Epigrams and proverbs are
kindred guidelines.

All is ever changing for the better or the worse.

To die is as common as it is to be born.

Nothing is ever quite what it ever was.

Morality guides and politics decides.

No one or other form of government suits and serves every country.

Good governments change their countries for the better, and astute countries alter their governments for the better.

Businesses entice and persuade and customers fall in line and keep in step.

The old are out, the young are in, and the world continues its rapid spin.

While the busy make hay, the indolent just bay.

Some exercise their bodies, others their brains,
The foolish do neither, and the wise do both.

Beauty does not tarry. It just glows then goes.

Philanthropy should not become an industry.

Hate is a fuel that pollutes as it rages.

Communism is a way of life, capitalism is a mode of business.

Good friends lighten one's burdens and brighten one's horizons.

An epigram a day will brighten your way.

British royalty has become a dolorous comedy.

Risk not, reap not.

Don't stand and wait, go and get.

Curb your want and feed your need.

Don't pout and shout, stake and take.

Some shake and bake, others just lounge and scrounge.

Slake your thirst and sate your hunger before you slumber.

Philosophy is not a corporate industry.

Well-being is western, Nirvana is eastern.

Humans have always fashioned their gods.

Politicized religion and social mayhem walk hand in hand.

Political poles too often serve particular political interests.

To find, it is necessary to search.

Humor hoodwinks taboo.

Adversity is not a tragedy.

Time is friend and foe.

To pen a couple of epigrams a day, does much to keep the doldrums at bay.

Animals in the wild are lean and mean, household pets are fat and friendly.

Children are at play every day and in every way.

The Ten Commandments have slowly become cultural flotsam and jetsam.

Human beings were not divinely created, but only evolved quite naturally.

Wishful thinking and pious hopes are palliative not cures.

The living don't just die, they are felled by time and circumstances.

Theocracies, autocracies, aristocracies and democracies et al, have had their day, now technocracies are coming our way.

Fats leave sated, sugars leave craving.

Time does not come and go, humans do.

God is the toiler and the devil is the spoiler.

Deeds are done, while words are but spun.

Blows break bones, slurs but sting.

Few are the humans not spent, rent and malcontent.

Neither gridlock nor compromise appeal to the wise.

Compromise mollifies more than it satisfies.

The death penalty is more vindication than solution.

Deception and violence change things for the worse and not for the better.

Religions are all well-intentioned. They abuse when misused.

Democracies are very laudable, but also very fallible.

Social and political questions abound, and their many answers do little more than astound.

Great nations build bridges, not walls.

Humanity will never accept itself for what it actually is.

Pulchritude does not and should not characterize female teachers.

I would if I could but I can't, is a popular chant.

The city lad knows more and does less, while the country lad knows less and does more.

Better an active mind and lazy body than an active body and a lazy mind.

To dine, wine and dance is often to begin a romance.

Who wants tiresome peace when there's exciting war to be had?

Facts are elusive and discomforting, surmise is at one's disposal and alleviating.

Peace and quiet are tranquilizer, a low; conflict and turmoil are adrenalin, a high.

What is too little for some is too much for others.

The death penalty is justice thwarted, not justice served.

The Roman Empire became Christianized and Christianity became Romanized.

Mankind's religions reveal more of mankind than of God.

In the Muslim world, religion and politics are joined at the hip.

Where money can be made, it will be made and regardless of negative consequences.

Time and space are perplexing cousin concepts.

Where there is less waste there is less need.

Convenience is a luxury, not a necessity.

The Kingdom of God is a wondrous figment of the imagination.

Onward Christian Soldiers has again become a battle call.

The black holes of astrophysics are description, not explanation.

It is conventionality and not individualism that makes a functioning, cohesive society possible.

The Imperium Americanum has become a yawn and an "O hum."

The U.S.A does not have the power, will or wisdom to repair what is broken in the Middle East.

Does the turmoil of the Middle East herald a biblical Armageddon, as some would hope or fear?

Human calamities are mostly of human making.

Humans are as destructive as they are constructive.

Evil lurks within and not without.

Most have as much reason to be positive as to be negative.

Decent humans are almost as rare as a hen's teeth.

Oh to be good just to be good.

Words propagate, ideas generate.

All that is and happens is but an endless flow of consequences.

Life is no less a wondrous agony than it is an agonizing wonder.

Toil heats the body and indolence warms the chair.

All that is, decays in time.

But for its many suns, the universe would be one vast black hole.

Society has its many humble tillers and toilers and its few august money managers.

To ignore the past and to be unmindful of the future is to be less than human.

We know there is an earth and wish there were a heaven.

Human behavior is in keeping with human nature.

Nothing begins but that it also ends.

It begins in a cradle and ends in a coffin.

Retaliation is born of anger and anger is born of retaliation.

God is a creation of man and man is a creation of God.

The wealthy should be giving and the poor should be given.

What better than a decent human being!

Romantic love is many things both good and bad.

Children are obligations, not possessions.

Idle hands are mischief prone.

Thinkers are more inclined to think than to do, and doers are more inclined to do than to think.

Snakes their skin slough off, parents their children send off.

Life is not intent upon hell or salvation but solely upon self-propagation.

Humans treat humans less humanely than they do their pet animals.

Thinkers are not born, they evolve.

Warm feelings keep alive, cold feelings leave limp.

To become a mother is short play, to be a mother is a long day.

Some kill to stay alive, others kill to thrive.

But for testosterone and estrogen, there'd be little dance and romance.

Despite technology's revitalization of our spent Western Judeo-Christian culture, its days are numbered.

But for estrogen, there'd be fewer young preening beauties and fewer dour old spinsters.

To kill for what is dying, is to kill for nil.

Help the living live, and let the dying die.

To loaf day after day is but to waste away.

What is sport but passion, vice and violence.

Royalty has had its day and should now just fade away.

Those who persist doggedly are rewarded handsomely.

Crown and throne have become but smile and groan.

One must do ought, not to become distraught.

To be happy is to be content, and to be content is to be happy.

But for testosterone, there'd be fewer gallant lovers and few bold
warriors.

The strong should be less assertive and the weak should be
less timid.

What does not die, has never lived.

Like flowers, cultures germinate, grow, blossom, seed, wither
and die.

Education broadens and training narrows.

A child is a tabula rasa, an adult is a fait accompli.

Nothing is as it once was.

Words like good and bad are more judgmental than descriptive.

Moderation is cautious investment and dependable returns.

The truth of the matter is that there are no absolute truths.

Learning is a process of absorption, integration, evaluation and
application, structured by memory, reason and imagination.

Science counters our human propensity to think but what we will
and want to think.

For all too many, life's a bicycle that has two flat tires.

To become wise in the ways and thought of mankind, you must yourself exhaust both body and mind.

Religions are born of need, sustained by wishful thinking and pious hope, then doomed by a culminating skepticism.

What is truth but that which is true.

We would be spirit and are but flesh.

Some limp though physically unimpaired.

The children of the rich and those of the poor live on different planets.

The have nots are no less human than the haves.

Just not to be bad is not to be good.

Good will and good deeds sow good seeds.

Life's rich fare of thought , deed and feeling, can leave one overwhelmed and reeling.

Those of a kind, readily bind.

Do not elect to neglect, inspect and correct.

Most ever hunger for ever more.

Protect and conserve, don't kill and preserve.

To squirm we never stop until we finally drop.

Life is need and pain, struggle and strain, and nothing is ever likely to change.

Education prepares for life, and training assures a livelihood.

The conventional is predictable and assures stability,
The exceptional is unpredictable and invites instability.

To learn we never stop until we finally drop.

The human lot is good cause for pensive pause.

To mediate is to deflate, to dictate is to inflate.

Problems are for the solving, facts are for the knowing.

Without our Goliaths, we'd have no Davids.

The familiar attracts, the foreign is cause for pause.

Intensities excite and exhaust.

Exuberance oft triggers flatulence.

Beauty is appearance, not essence.

To define intelligence is a daunting challenge for the most intelligent.

War makes more money than peace. Ergo.

One must know sorrow to know joy.

Ubiquitous despair, fear and rage tell the story of our age.

Hope for helping hands, don't expect them.

Hope and chance our lives enhance.

Dialogue that infuriates rather than informs is dialogue that is derelict.

Nothing is somewhere, anywhere, everywhere, or even nowhere.

Some are choice, some chance, and others accident, but all are wondrous possibility.

Every dance is a romance.

For some, life is a "Welcome," for others an "At your own Risk."

Like night the day, repose and recovery will follow exertion and exhaustion.

Home is an attachment, not a place.

Our friends and enemies are but chance and choice.

To survive, spare the chicken and eat the eggs.

Learn to swim or build a bridge.

Our world's stage is plagued by fear, despair and rage.

Men are intrinsically highly-sexed hunters and warriors, while women are naturally accommodating wives and mothers.

Evolution has been life's resolution.

Nature is of God and culture is of man.

Heaven is harmony, earth is cacophony.

All does not begin with birth and all does not end with death.

Humans are not just male or female, but varying blends of the two possibilities.

Doers do and thinkers think, and rarely the twain does ever meet.

"I would if I could, but I can't" is an all too common rant.

The present is immediacy and poignancy, the past but faint memory and the future but vague hope.

Home is within and not without.

Our holidays are shopping days, and not the holy days that they once were.

Not to address cause is not to achieve cure.

It is primarily the face that projects the person.

In fulfillment, possibility becomes reality.

Too many acorns never become oaks.

Life's challenge is to become the possibility that it is.

"Law and Order" is a possibility, "Freedom and Order" is
   pious hope.

Possibility is elusive, probability is seductive.

To teach but what to think is but to indoctrinate.

Virtuality has become the digital world's actuality.

Beauty spots are salvaged blemishes.

Loud protests are screams for help.

Love is a two-edged sword.

Broadly to inform and to nurture critical thought, is to educate.

Human beings are astounding possibility and wanting reality.

Too many are too little the possibility that they were.

Government should do what the individual cannot do.

Expectations can be spur or burr.

Hate taints both hater and hated.

Don't sedate grief, let it slowly abate.

Denigration is reduction, appreciation is affirmation.

Technology's obsessive preoccupation with things, has trivialized
   both life and human beings.

Of this be certain: Hate invites hate, and love invites love.

Life's what, whence, whither and why, the human mind will
   ever defy.

Evolution is adjustment not solution.

Hiroshima and Nagasaki, the epitome of inhumanity.

Set your sight on what is right.

Health trumps wealth.

Grunt, don't grumble.

Something is wrong when nothing is right.

Take what is yours but never by force.

Cultivate sagacity and control rapacity.

Your depth is more important than your height.

Belief and relief go hand in hand.

To avoid death, avoid birth.

Spitters infect others and swallowers infect themselves.

Slackers and quitters are of a common kind.

The hypersensitive self-effacing are self-tormenters.

Humans and guns are a match made in hell.

Time and space are the vast nothingness that envelops all change.

Females tend to stay, males are inclined to stray.

Too many are but frozen frowns and too few are radiant smiles.

Work and play are but judgment, not fixed reality.

Where there is no change, there is no time.

Where there is nothing, there is no space.

Sight, sound, taste, smell and touch are consequences of
    experiences and not things.

When upset, don't stew and fret, take an exhausting walk.

To know too much can paralyze, to know too little can neutralize.

Yesterday's necessities become today's curiosities.

Nothing is, all is ever shrinking or expanding.

Horses, once necessities, are today but quaint curiosities.

The virtually dead are actually alive.

Togetherness is escape and comfort.

Life is victim, death is victor.

To drift with the wind is for the birds.

Prepare before you dare.

Effort is as rewarding as it is demanding.

Automation is liberation.

Fraud diminishes no less than it benefits.

The feckless disturb, the reckless perturb.

Blows can lame physically, and words can maim psychologically.

To remember selectively is to smile contentedly.

Unburdening the self oft burdens others.

Life does and death undoes.

Scams have become a common business practice.

To test is to bring out the best.

Effort absolves and resolves.

Theft diminishes both victim and perpetrator.

Heed, and you will be heeded.

Where there is hope, there is light, and where there is light, there
is sight.

Despair, fear and rage tell the story of our age.

Given to things, one becomes a thing.

We look nostalgically to the past, and anxiously to the future.

Fear animates the brave and intimidates the cowardly.

We come empty-handed and leave empty-handed. Is all of nought?

We flay and pray that things will go our way.

The many come and go, and leave no trace behind.

Tears, toil, hope and endurance are life's very substance.

Good or bad, rich or poor, we all leave as naked as we came.

Death is but the final of life's plethora of changes.

Nothing is as it was or will be.

Let stray what will not stay.

One is as fortunate as one is unfortunate.

One loves and hates what seems to be the case.

Curb feelings and spur thoughts.

To argue infallibility is to argue advantage.

A smile can conceal as much as it can reveal.

Money has become master. It dictates.

The Commandments are imperatives, not requests.

Women display, men prefer to play.

Men would rule the roost, women warm the hearth.

The tried and true are far too few.

Just to kneel and pray will not save the day.

Patience is reflective, impetuosity is reflexive.

Talent is lauded, decency is embraced.

The female is agent, the male but adjunct.

Some act regardless of consequences, others do not act for fear of consequences.

There are those who are ever ready and those who are never ready.

Some never have their fill of swill.

Adversity can be challenge and opportunity.

Chutzpah is brazen affront, ego on display.

Mankind is no less destructive than it is constructive.

Dramatize to better advertize.

Life proposes and fate disposes.

Too much talk is as bad as too little talk.

Hear and heed, don't shout and flout.

To forbid is both to annoy and to whet the appetite.

When private interest trumps the commonweal, democracies begin to reel.

Better to shake hands than to point fingers.

People live with what is, and change is slow in its coming.

Facts are verifiable, truths need no verification.

When private interests trump the commonweal, democracies begin to reel.

Some are a whole, while many more are but a part of a whole.

Integrity, humility, generosity and dignity spell humanity.

Prejudice simplifies life but it fosters strife.

To think, to feel and to do, is to be.

Dreams are but reality transmogrified in light sleep.

But that we fear, we would not be here.

There can be too much of a good thing.

Books bask in their author's shadow.

To write about others is to write about oneself.

To know better is to appreciate more.

A feather must be fixed or it will blow.

Language is more suggestion and approximation than it is clarity
and precision.

Teachers give and students take and make.

Writers go where readers fear to tread.

Too little novelty is to tease, and too much novelty is to tax.

Reading is for the receptive ready.

The driven write, to their readers' delight.

Writers and readers are flip sides of the same coin.

Writers relieve themselves and readers burden themselves.

Reading is no less cathartic than is writing.

To know no want is to have no wants.

Marriages have become temporarily permanent.

Writing is release and reading is increase.

What writers know, readers want to know.

The Ten Commandments are honored in their breech.

Marriage, once a revered sacrament, has become but one of life's many temporary wayside stations.

To come to grips and to terms with self and with life is both responsibility and challenge.

Gratitude improves mood.

Please liberally and appease sparingly.

We are but flesh and would-be spirit.

We are given to life but doomed to die.

Not to be ought, is to be a nought.

Peer at the past to prepare for the future.

Look backward before you look forward.

Time is a measure of change, and not something that changes.

Violence is born of weakness and not of strength.

Touted masculinity has always been less sublimity than asininity.

Sex generates life and food perpetuates it.

Where there are no differences of opinion, there are no opinions.

Unwarranted expectations and unsolicited advice are all too often more pain than gain.

Juvenile mentalities are shaping today's realities.

To sing and to dance is life to enhance.

To know little is to do little.

Though lame of body, one can be game of mind.

To believe is to achieve.

Taxes tax too many of the taxed.

There are those who try and do, and then there are those who but try to do.

Wealth is a goal that takes its toll.

Philosophers are not chimney sweeps.

Consensus is means, not solution.

Earth is for the living, heaven is for the dead.

Love is treasured by some and purchased by others.

Love dilates the heart, anger dilates the arteries.

Stasis can be an oasis in a world of hectic change.

To please, don't tease.

Humanity resounds when calamity abounds.

Genes and life-style spell brevity or longevity.

Earth embraces the living and Heaven welcomes the dead.

To see, you must first look.

Wall Street is economy-minded but psychology-moved.

The rich have all they want, the poor but suffer want.

When the good quail, the bad prevail.

Comply or die has become a battle cry.

When the lawless rule the roost, the law's in need of a real boost.

The rich have pockets deep, the poor have heavy hearts.

To be different is not to be defective.

The rich have much and want yet more.

To know oneself is to know the other.

Would that we could but set like the sun.

Would that we could when we can't.

The rich will have their day, the poor are left to bray.

Commonalities bind, differences grind.

Inhumanity spawns inhumanity.

The strong know no wrong, and the weak are too meek to speak.

Today's awesome digital novelties will be tomorrow's dusty antiquities.

Entertainment and attraction have become a serious seduction.

Spend if you must, but don't go bust.

Heed and help when help is needed.

Truth is ideology, lies are reality.

Most causes are more demanding than rewarding.

Makers are shakers and breakers.

Trust has world-wide flown the coop, and distrust has settled in.

Automation is changing the face of every nation.

Winners wag their tails and losers lick their wounds.

Men are roamers and women are homers.

A measure of leisure is a measure of pleasure.

Rodents will survive and cats will thrive.

Indolence is offensive and expensive.

Anarchy is freedom gone berserk.

Culturally, all that has been done will, in due time, be undone.

Soundbites are the currency of politics.

Prescriptions fuel addictions.

A temper is pollution not solution.

Lightning startles, thunder rattles.

Hurry, all too often ends in flurry.

The pragmatic focus on the possible, the idealistic, on the impossible.

Expect and respect differences of opinion.

To meet halfway can carry the day.

Belief is to feel and truth is to know.

Thank you, I'm sorry, and Please, are words that appease.

Good health elates, poor health grates.

Singles are flint and fire, the married are kith and kin.

But to taste is a waste.

Marriage is a mutual "give and take," and not a singular "I take and you give."

Power should be given, and not taken.

The body moves, the mind cultivates.

Our tomorrows inherit our todays.

Never kill, let live and die.

Any fool can distort the Golden Rule.

Giving is a gift shared by all too few.

Roads go nowhere. They just begin and end.

Reason curbs the emotions and the emotions compromise reason.

It begins with psychology and ends with psychology, thoughts to the contrary notwithstanding.

Home is a concept, not a house.

Too many tomorrows are but yesterdays.

Prevention is better than remedial attention.

To become a sage, you must fully live and slowly age.

The hapless, helpless and the hopeless, wallow in their chronic distress.

The many are in and of our radically-changing world, the few are in but no longer of it.

Language and political purpose: Criminals have become terrorists, and criminality has become terrorism.

The world is politically bleak and promises to become bleaker.

What was forbidden yesterday, is tolerated today, and will be acceptable tomorrow.

Questions demand answers and answers spawn questions, and ne'er mankind's curiosity will wane.

Sex hexes as much as it flexes.

It is difference that makes the difference.

Storytellers do not lie, they fabricate.

Self-absorption is self-distortion.

Many who know won't tell, and those who don't know, can't.

Of the living, too many are less alive than dead.

Sport was a game that became an industry.

The mental and the physical are of a kind, but rarely of like mind.

The able are not always the willing, and the willing are not always the able.

A house is a nest, an apartment building is a beehive.

Self-realization is contingent upon self-experience and self-knowledge.

Wall Street is manic and Main Street is depressed.

A fallow mind, like a fallow field, has no yield.

Better to have driverless cars than to have headless drivers.

Legality compels and morality constrains.

Adulation is nauseation.

For some, work never ends, and play never starts.

Too many love too little and hate too much.

The world has always been too much for some and too little for others.

The younger would be older and the older would be younger.

Don't run if you needn't walk.

Repetition is not correction.

In a house without a bible, the devil has no rival.

The dead will rise when two and two is five.

Wall Street is sated and Main Street is emaciated.

Motherhood is more learning than instinct.

A couple of epigrams a day will keep doldrums away.

Expectation knows frustration.

Competitors do battle, they don't make love.

Poetry's rhymes are veritable chimes.

To be given to the past is to short change the future.

To befriend is better than to offend.

To know can devastate no less than elate.

Success should not inflate, and failure should not deflate.

Unfettered capitalism spells unfettered corruption.

Like the wealthy, the poor are both good and bad.

Poetry cuts to the quick and more.

Many are of a kind, few are of a mind.

Humans know much, but comprehend little.

Activity is universal, action is particular.

When the hounds bay, the hunted flee the fray.

Women are in love with love and need to be loved.

Poetry touches the heart and soul, prose addresses the mind.

The shapers are few and the shaped are many.

Some have a heart, others have a purse.

Paucity is resentment and abundance is contentment.

People of a kind are not necessarily of one mind.

Forgive and forget without rancor or regret.

Birds of a kind each other find.

What can be said of one can be said of another.

Sing in spring and let it ring.

Those who confide are likely to abide.

Law protects and compels.

One person's contentment is another person's resentment.

All that's done by everyone, is directly or indirectly motivated by the drive to stay alive.

Words touch, actions grip.

Difference should excite and not distress.

A cold shower energizes, a hot bath lethargizes.

Neither time nor space can be packaged and marketed.

To give up liberty for security is to invite rank tyranny.

The brawny are rarely brainy, and the brainy are rarely brawny.

The strong can't be wrong by definition.

To help another in one way is to help oneself in another way.

People do what they do because they are what they are.

Regrets are lessons not punishment.

Lemons, champagne do not make.

Brawn is to brain what water is to oil.

A house becomes a home, when its dwellers cease to roam.

Not to greet when we meet is less than meet.

Sex is mankind's call of the wild.

To kill is to be the lesser for it.

Life does not have a roadmap.

Money cannot atone for the damage money does.

Change exhilarates and change decimates.

Word-learning is most ready in contextual repetition, least ready in simple repetition.

Limited minds have limited visions.

Distraction both alerts and disrupts.

It is not meet to bleat.

Head is master, stomach is servant.

Some run until they're done, and some are done before they run.

Being is becoming and becoming is being.

It is no surprise that a beautiful oriental rug is a feast for the eyes.

No change, no time; no things, no space.

Individual privacy and the public's security need not be at loggerheads.

Sage rhymes with age.

To rant and to rave is but to pant and to crave.

Religion dwells on God and morality dwells on humans.

Knowledge and skill coffers will fill.

Instability makes for anxiety and fragility.

Mental weakness bumbles, physical weakness stumbles.

Egocentricity is nature and altruism is culture.

Moralists scold and correct, philosophers pause and reflect.

Depression is warning and challenge.

Each is accountable for more than each would acknowledge.

Better to be empty than to be full of oneself.

A dull mind has no sharp edges.

Political rhetoric is deflective and not corrective.

The Black Community is a problem, the White Community is the problem.

Resolve, don't revenge.

Lack of self-love contaminates other-love.

Other-anger is all too often but deflected self-anger.

Rats play hide, cats play seek, and right often they do meet.

To curb wants and to heed needs is to be in control and not to be controlled.

Sticks and stones bruise physically, and untoward words bruise psychologically.

Nothing learned is learned in vain.

Belief assuages all grief.

The wealthy want, the poor need.

Luxuries are not necessities.

The common necessities of the wealthy are the rare luxuries of the poor.

Egocentricity is not an eccentricity.

Bullies are sting- and not honey- bees.

The Electronics Age is less taken with humans than given to things.

One person's luxuries are another person's necessities.

To try is to fail or to succeed and not to try is but to fail.

Silence invites reflection and chatter leads to commotion.

What are indispensables to some are dispensables to others.

We know that we know little, and that that little is suspect.

The exceptional are different, and their difference makes a
difference.

When everybody is empowered, no one is in charge.

Life can become precarious when freedom becomes imperious.

Each is both beneficiary and victim of his/her own beliefs.

There is always more than meets the eye.

Too many people are but living cadavers.

More can be little and little can be more.

Speed spells more things from birth to death.

Opposites and similar, can both attract and repel.

Dreams realized are dreams sullied.

Shoot not to kill but to hone your skill.

Privacy is desire, security is must.

Work is play for some, and play is work for others.

Religion is belief and morality is behavior.

Mind is the I, and body is the self.

Shallow waters teem with life.

Fallow fields seed themselves.

The empty ring hollow.

Becoming is life's constant.

Feet accommodate both slow and fleet.

Heaven and Hell are Christianity's carrot and club.

Fear should be treasured, not feared.

Better to be partly right than wholly wrong.

Digital addiction can become an affliction.

Tighten your belt or you will lose your pants.

We live by lies and myth and all parades as truth.

Sagacity, unlike rapacity, is beyond most people's capacity.

Reason is all too often more self-serving than truth-finding.

Necessities and not luxuries should be our priorities.

Every romance is but a dance of chance.

Peace is anaemic while war is bulimic.

To invoke divine authority is to abdicate responsibility.

To go along to get along is expediency not morality.

The corpulent should curb, not carb their appetites.

The pillars of piety are no less corrupt than the pillars of society.

Life is but a bewildering hiatus between womb and tomb.

Love demands dark rich soil and caring hands.

A person frail of heart has lost before the start.

Truth is no more and no less than invention become convention.

It's not what your body is, but what your person does.

Some are at their best when they protest.

Bullies are deviant would-bes.

Our todays are blessed and burdened by our yesterdays.

Humans mouth virtues and enjoy their vices.

Truths and lies are no more than social necessities.

The truth of reality is best exposed by the lie of literature.

Life's imponderables are pondered by life's cripples.

The arrogance of the informed is equaled only by the ignorance of the uninformed.

Metaphors are poetry and not argument.

In the end, all ends in a gasp of despair or in a desperate hope.

Youth's pursuit of truth is age's preference of wisdom.

Truths make life worthwhile and lies make it possible.

Uncertainties may be our only certainties.

If there are no absolutes, then relativity too is relative.

A fact can be established, truth only argued.

The possessed possess this world of ours.

Every truth will have its day, but none is ever here to stay

Fear of failure is one of the many seeds of success.

Love blesses both giver and receiver.

The practical and the beautiful are at their best when wedded.

Learn how to live and you will learn how to die.

Comics don't laugh, they only make people laugh.

Yesterday's solutions are often today's problems.

Men dress conventionally, women intentionally.

Many are good because they are too weak to be bad.

Virtuality diminishes actuality.

Mankind will never cease refashioning what God fashioned.

Religions decry the present and look forward to the future.

Rare is the person who goes gently into that good night.

Love humanizes, pain strengthens and faith calms.

Truth is no less mortal than its thinkers.

It never rains but that it stops.

Feelings and emotions are their own reward and punishment.

Humanity, liberty and democracy do not pop out of the barrels of guns.

Information without judgment is a pile of bricks without a builder.

Brains not used are brains abused.

A tool not sharpened but used, is a tool not appreciated but abused.

The weak should be strong and the strong should be magnanimous.

When expediency prevails, morality pales.

We come as bundles of potentialities and leave as bundles of bones

Hope and despair are choice not lot.

Modesty elevates socially, deprecates personally.

Pain and shame are salutary torment.

We are both blessed and blighted by our forebears.

No one is beyond the wear and tear of time and care.

Once you know the other, you will know that he is your brother.

When it rains, it always pours or never rains enough.

Truth is a constant becoming.

There are those who would if they could, and those who could if they would.

The most gifted are often the most blighted.

Life is a private ecstasy and agony.

Chastity is cherished, promiscuity is practised.

Integrity is trumpeted, deception is practised.

The American dream is becoming the world's nightmare.

Happiness is as fleeting as a beautiful sunset.

It is not good enough just to feed the hungry.

A tasty dish becomes a stinking pile of excrement.

A meeting of minds is most likely when there's a meeting of hearts.

To ask the right question is as important as to give the right answer.

Deception diminishes both deceiver and deceived.

Curb your appetite or it will curb you.

Moderation is not a deprivation.

Responsibility is a homing pigeon.

Exposure to too much leaves one with too little.

Better to be partly right than to be wholly wrong.

Equality in opportunity is legality and morality, equality in rewards is sheer inanity.

Some friends are not worth their price.

Pithy sayings are aesthetically pleasing and intellectually teasing.

We think what we think, do what we do and feel what we feel, because we are what we are.

To hate is as natural as to love.

Aloneness is existential fact, loneliness is personal choice.

Celebrate the possible, don't just mourn the impossible.

Too many people who make it are themselves unmade in the making.

To be more curious is to live more intensely.

We do not live by bread alone, we live by lies.

Emoting has its place, but so does thinking.

Only some of the rich are bad, and only some of the poor are good.

It's nice to be important, but it is more important to be nice.

Never squeeze a sneeze, you may leave a calling card.

Focus on the battle and the war will take care of itself.

Consequences should be forethought, not afterthought.

Friction generates more heat than light.

Speeches can electrify the world, it takes action to rewire it.

Expectation knows more grief than exhilaration.

Those uncomfortable with others are essentially uncomfortable with the self.

One day leads but to another, and each is as novel as the other.

Slogans and labels don't elucidate, they obfuscate.

When morality takes wing, meism has its fling.

Accept what cannot be changed, and change what cannot be accepted.

Hesitate and cogitate before you bloviate.

Give generously and take discreetly.

We bruise easily and heal slowly.

Every pain and every pleasure duly spaced and in due measure.

Distraction is the troubled mind's attraction.

There's much delight where there's little oversight.

Einstein was appalled by what he called the infinity of human stupidity.

Most live in the world of opinion and not in the world of reflection

Freedom is less gift or right than it is challenge and opportunity.

Wars have had their day. It's time for diplomacy to have its say.

Power is commonly abused and for good but rarely used.

Do your best, and to God leave the rest.

A tempered tête-à-tête is much more effective than a temper tantrum.

Too many definitions opine more than they define.

Gossip and rumor are hardy seeds that spread and grow like noxious weeds.

Religions are born of need and fashioned by the imagination.

Religion is God-centered, morality is man-centered.

Men keep things on edge, women quiet things down.

Diplomacy is a two-way street, not a one-way highway.

Ours is a disconnected connectedness! Thanks to the Electronics Age.

Religions both enlighten and blind.

If corruption is possible, corruption will occur, and corruption is always possible.

Religious divides are more enduring and no less devastating than political divides.

Be grateful for the done, and don't harp upon the undone.

Innovation in moderation is our salvation.

Work with zest and then rest.

The many have too little choice, the few, too much.

Newspapers advocate too much and report too little.

Reason is commonly more self-serving than truth-finding.

Necessities and not luxuries should be our priorities.

Pursue your passions with passion.

Too many believe what they want to believe and what serves their purposes.

America talks democracy and walks plutocracy.

Everybody's cup of tea is not everybody's cup of tea.

Life can become precarious when freedom becomes imperious.

Most people are not good or bad, but both good and bad, and hopefully more good than bad.

Freedom binds to the degree that it unshackles.

Reasoning leads to conclusions, emotions lead to action.

In a commodity culture, human beings become but another commodity.

Our Electronics Age is a thing and not thought culture.

Delinquent juveniles and adult criminals are birds of a feather.

For many, change is an unsettling progression from the known to the unknown.

Only a blessed few leave imprints that recall them.

Peace and war are foretastes of heaven and hell.

The music of the heavenly spheres is beyond our earthly ears.

Humanism had its cultural day, technology now holds sway.

Financial and political manipulation has become an abomination.

Peace is anaemic, war is bulimic.

When belief wanes and dies, its culture does likewise.

To invoke divine authority is to abdicate responsibility.

To focus on differences is to stoke animosities.

Our emotional lives are primary, our intellectual lives are secondary.

Convictions and beliefs are generally long in their making, and just as long in their unmaking.

The genders are both attracted to, and suspicious of each other.

Genius is a rare abnormality, a wondrous deviation from the norm.

Life's sole interest is self-perpetuation, and life's sole purpose is to beget more life.

There is little that the human being cannot justify.

Thought is deliberate, emotions are reflexive.

Aloneness is a physical fact, loneliness is a psychological state.

Love endears and will compels.

Greed has little to do with need.

Women tend to internalize and men are inclined to externalize.

Expectations mother a turmoil of emotions.

The more involved in decision making, the fewer the decisions.

Outlaws shoot from the hip, politicians shoot from the lip.

The way to get along is to go along, and that's plain wrong.

Most people do not think, let alone think about their thought.

To win at whatever and whatever cost, has become a common modus operandi.

Killing is too high a price for killing.

Women have always been victims and martyrs.

Too many are too busy doing nothing to do something.

Minor adjustments can often make for major changes.

In a thing culture, humans themselves become things.

War is too high a price for peace.

Say what exhilarates and not what denigrates.

Anger is reaction, not resolution.

Boys are given to their toys, and girls are taken with their pearls.

Head and heart should fall in line and keep in step.

Too many are taken with goods, and too few are given to goodness.

To go along to get along is expediency not morality.

To emote less and to reflect more will preclude much verbal war.

Democracy is moral, capitalism is amoral.

To work is a gain, to become one's work is a loss.

The corpulent should curb, not carb their appetite.

Digital togetherness and aloneness go hand in hand.

Democracy is people-minded, capitalism is money-mad.

Physical and mental health are dependent upon financial wealth.

Virtuality takes from reality as much as it adds to it.

The sage has learned to settle for less.

Privacy has become a luxury of the past.

Too many make excuses, too few make commitments.

Too many are too busy getting nowhere.

Apps are as much curiosities as they are amenities.

Memories are painting not photographs.

History is as much fiction as it is fact.

Military victories are more loss than gain, and less joy than pain.

Big bang, black holes and dark matter are more gothic fiction
than hard science.

Noblesse oblige is an adage foreign to the corporate world.

Much in human affairs might better end before it begins.

Expediency is an incidental antidote not a tried cure.

Nationalism knew retribution, globalization knows reciprocity.

Retribution stokes, reconciliation banks.

The exceptional are society's gain and pain.

Life is a tangle of proprieties and improprieties.

Unanimity is a rare reality.

Individuals are as different mentally as they are physically.

The harried and hurried have little time for leisure and pleasure.

Enchanting dreamers often become disenchanted recluses.

Capitalism and inequality are synonymous.

What can't be cured, must be endured.

To break it, is to own it.

It is tenacity that separates the exceptional and the ordinary.

To admit one's ignorance is to know one's limits.

Objectivity is but banked subjectivity.

It begins with the self and ends with the self, and all else is dressing.

Writers clarify life's muddy waters.

To cure is good, to prevent is better.

To do nothing is to do nothing good, but also to do nothing bad.

Classroom clowns become national comedians.

Present-day rowdyism could benefit from a touch of old-time quietism.

Politics has always been a popular power pursuit.

Humans given to things, become things.

Like the Industrial Revolution, the Electronics Age will change the world both for the better and the worse.

Both Islam and Christianity are rent and spent.

Artificial intelligence will supplement, not supplant, human intelligence.

To adapt or not to adapt is to flourish or to perish.

Fear both unites and separates.

Love and hate are life's major thrusts.

Writing is born of life, imagination, skill and need.

Struggle for the good is its own reward.

Conviction is the beginning of friction.

Writing is compulsive, agony and bliss, and is rewarding to both writer and reader.

Thought agitates, work enervates and indolence sedates.

The Athenians of old were brain and right, the Spartans were brawn and fight.

Disease care is incidental, health care is fundamental.

Skills pay bills.

Paranoia both plagues and guarantees survival.

Action is trying, inertia is deadening.

The few talk and demand, the many listen and oblige.

To survive and to flourish, both institutions and individuals have always had recourse to a plethora of questionable self-serving games.

There has always been a heavenly retreat for the humble, the weak and the meek.

A tired old Humanism yielded effetely to a compelling vigorous youthful Technology.

To the delight of the male, a hysterectomy absents the baby carriage but leaves the playpen intact.

Cultures wither and die, only to take wing anew and to soar high.

Lives are less predictable than they are accountable.

Life's land mines can be as devastating as actual land mines.

Change for the better, yes; change for the thrill, no!

Physical punishment serves no good purpose.

If not right, stay out of sight.

It pays to be tough when the going's rough.

Never to be wrong is rarely to be right.

Goodwill is contagious and smiles beget smiles.

Kind seeks it kind.

To preen is to keep clean.

Togetherness is heavenliness.

To racially profile is to revile.

Anti-Zionism invites anti-Semitism.

Self-exhibition is a common inclination.

Corporal punishment spells pain void of gain.

To observe is to preserve.

Love relationships are vulnerable, friendships are durable.

Choose to win and not to lose.

Strive to win and prepare to lose.

Be young in spirit though old in body.

Drugs counter afflictions but also invite addictions.

Philosophy expounds, it does not solve.

Life is lived, not solved.

Though unreal, all heavenly abodes appeal.

Too little thought is inanity, too much thought is insanity.

Play, like work, must have its day.

Preventative care will be tomorrow's medical order of the day.

The humble poor kow-tow, the haughty rich strut and stare.

Love won't go away, and hate is here to stay.

Truth lurks dark and deep in every soul.

Haste means waste, and waste is bad taste.

To keep on squirming is to keep on learning.

To have roots, we need to read.

Stress invites distress.

It's this way below because it's that way above.

Not to first taste, is a waste.

The rich have wealth to spare and power to bare.

The poor have but poverty to share and suffering to bear.

To live no life is to die no death.

Hectic hurry invites confusing flurry.

To show is to inform, to display is to impress.

Timidity is uncertainty, brashness is rashness.

The past had its day, the future will have its way.

To learn one never ceases until death one releases.

But to berate will but stir hate.

Where there's no thinking, there's no thought.

Ideality is the idealist's reality.

Reality is painful fact, ideality is soothing fiction.

Where there's no welcome, there's no farewell.

Common sense is not as common as it purports to be.

Palliatives are as common as panaceas are scarce.

Avoid battle when possible, do battle when necessary.

One may not lose when one does not win.

Winners are often losers, and losers are often winners.

Paradox is fact, not fiction.

Fight or flight, the choice is yours.

Some do, some think, some do both and some do neither.

Morality is reward and punishment.

Moderation is salvation.

Hate reduces and love seduces.

Hate is good for neither hater nor hated.

War is politics at its worst.

Political extremism is self-minded, not liberty-serving.

Tend to your own warts and tolerate those of others.

Most romances are but happenstances.

The tolerant are sure-footed, the intolerant are club-footed.

A push will attract a shove.

Aught ever becomes naught.

The intolerant are strident, the tolerant are silent.

Boys have too little poise and make too much noise.

Heed your need and tweak your greed.

The strong snarl, the weak whimper.

What is not broken need not be fixed.

Rights fly high and responsibilities lie low.

A life without purpose is movement without direction.

Most grow old and a few grow wise.

Some grow up and too many just grow.

Good will is a lubricant, ill will, an abrasive.

Head and heart should never part.

Be big-hearted, not small-minded.

Hear and heed those in need.

Mankind is potentially wise and actually foolish.

Even nobody is a somebody.

Man is something of his maker and more of his tempter.

Difference is to be appreciated, not denigrated.

Disagree, but do so without being disagreeable.

No animal is more creative or less destructive than the
human being.

To follow the money is to track criminality.

Peace through strength is pious hope.

Each stage of life leaves its indelible traces.

Reason proposes, emotion disposes.

Where there's a Juliet, there's a Romeo.

Flowers are a delight, and weeds a blight.

Brawn builds and brain transforms.

Moderation is challenge, indulgence is seduction.

Reason confines and sex binds.

To be human is to suffer and to dream of better possibility.

Disappointment lurks on the horizon of every undertaking.

Mankind opened the gate of hell as surely as it opened the portals of heaven.

To fail is to have tried.

Better self esteem than public acclaim.

The famous too often make a profession of their fame.

Choice is a choice possibility.

When there's no pain, there's no gain.

Resentment knows no contentment

Retribution, yes; retaliation, no!

Harmony is our god, cacophony is our lot.

To be good is good, to do good is better.

Earn what you get and get what you earn.

We should all be in a hurry not to be in a hurry.

Life is more cacophony than harmony.

Death is life's tomorrow.

Some are thinkers, others are doers, too many are neither and too few are both.

Look backward before you move forward.

One cannot give away what one does not have.

Words conceal no less than they reveal.

Few are levers, most are but cogs.

The quick are nimble, the fast are strong.

Fate is mankind's ultimate scapegoat.

Where there's sex, there's life.

Love not shown is love not known.

Life is everything that is good and everything that is bad.

Love is a gift and not a commodity.

We think truths and live lies.

Death's shadow looms larger than life.

Sex will hex and vex.

No one is a nobody.

Even the same have their differences.

Wall Street flourishes while Main Street languishes.

The same have their differences no less than the different.

The actual is tedious common place, the hyperbolic is dramatic possibility.

Idealism is of the parlor, realism is of the workshop.

Permanence is life's passion, evanescence is life's lot.

Life is a workday for the many, a playday for the few.

The harder one works, the luckier one gets.

The hoi polloi sweats, the hoity-toity perspires.

Longevity is our hope and brevity is our given.

To expect the unexpected is to be more sage than fool.

What is thought is private, what is said is public.

Hands that work are no less indispensable that minds that work.

The sinner-saint trafficked with Lucifer and opted for God.

A warm nest assures a good rest.

Life is as fractured as humans are flawed.

What God espouses, the devil disparages.

Activity is invigorating indolence is debilitating.

Rest is best after concerns have been addressed

All too few trail echoes or cast shadows.

Be yourself and not what others would have you be.

To help another is to be a sister or a brother.

No option, no bravery.

The familiar is common, the known is rare.

Too many solve problems by avoiding problems.

The more we think, the less we know.

Not to be given to thought is not to be plagued.

We thrash and flail and all to little avail.

Philosophers are by and large a distraught and unhappy lot.

A treat for the fleet and but woe for the slow.

Turn on the heat, don't just bleat.

The diligent add, the indolent subtract.

Think positively and do meticulously.

Not to live one's belief is not to believe.

Love is chance and dance, marriage is toil and roil.

Work can be play and play can be work.

Work taxes and play relaxes.

To stay at the top is not less demanding than to rise to the top.

To appreciate is to acknowledge and to approve.

To husband your means and to mend your ways is to brighten
    your future days.

Excess destroys itself.

But few private sparks ignite pubic passions.

To keep abreast requires some zest.

The blessed in spirit are the best in life.

To rage is anything but sage.

Ever to begin anew is but ever to self-renew.

Hypocrisy is a common commodity.

All is, ultimately, but an exercise in futility.

Freedom opens both the doors of heaven and of hell.

A lie is not a lie but that it is deliberate.

Tangle verbally, tango physically.

Cerebration is taxing, celebration is relaxing.

Earth is strife and lamentation, heaven is harmony and celebration.

Hell has more housing problems than does heaven.

Few have more and many have less.

Sages are not given to rages.

Failure precedeth success.

For the few, life is leisure and pleasure, for the many, life is work and worry.

The tired are physically weary and the weary are psychologically tired.

A hollow is but an inverted hill.

Some please wherever they are, others please whenever they leave.

Aloneness is a universal, loneliness is a particular.

Time is kind to neither body nor mind.

Integrity and respect have gone the way of dress and of deportment.

Timidity is retreat, temerity is attack.

Rest is best when rent and spent.

The strong take and the weak quake.

Money can do as much to you as for you.

Infidelity thy name is ubiquity.

Much that is lawful is right awful.

Good will does not kill.

The iniquitous are ubiquitous.

To do something is to be someone.

Shame on those who would shame others.

To do evil is to be evil.

A fact rarely remains intact.

To find a brother, appreciate the other.

Fate is universal, chance is particular.

Better an open than a closed mind.

Mankind has learned to kill with ever greater skill.

Tend to your own wants and tolerate another's.

Those of a kind, find that kind.

Thoughts spawn thoughts.

Better to make than to break.

Most do not repent until they're spent.

When rent and spent, relent and repent.

To win is often to lose.

The resolute persist, the astute insist.

When morality is suspended, society is upended.

Opinion is comfort, thought is discomfort.

Talkers outtalk and doers outdo.

The richer the rich, the poorer the poor.

Dream is fancy, life is fact.

Fear invites flight, anger incites fight.

One man's flow is another man's ebb.

Brain or brawn, the choice is yours.

Sunrise energizes, sunset lethargizes.

One may not be bad though one is not good.

God created the world and man refashioned it.

The dead remind, the living complain.

Don't pass by indifferently, go through receptively.

Religions are ennobling noble fictions.

Vanity knows no modesty.

We learn little when we win and much more when we lose.

Nothing ventured, nothing learned or gained.

The vain have much to lose and little to gain.

History feeds on slanted truths and outright lies.

To learn to know another is to find a sister or a brother.

Modesty is self-deflating and vanity is self-inflating.

Freedom of speech is fun and folly.

An addiction is an affliction that knows no satiation.

Money is a convenient means and a regrettable end.

Expect the possible, not the impossible.

Birth is painful and messy, life is a painful mess, and death is
    painful and messy.

To do nothing is to be nothing.

From nothingness to nothingness, and trying life between.

Death is the price of life.

Too many are too little more than the sum of their parts.

Integrity has become a scarcity.

Tedium lethargizes, interest energizes.

The ought of life becomes the nought of death.

Though small, one can stand tall.

Hypocrites are two-faced twits.

Epigrams have a point and can be sharp.

When emotion flows, reason ebbs.

To fare well is to feel good.

Retaliation is reflexive, rehabilitation is reflective.

A pensive pause is a good cause.

About the Author

Joseph Mileck was born in Sanktmar-tin, Roumania in 1922, immigrated to Canada in 1926 and again in 1931. He has a B.A. Degree from McMaster University, Hamilton, Ontario (1945), and a PhD. from Harvard University (1950). Joseph was a member of the German Department of the University of California, Berkeley from 1950 to 1991. He has published five books and numerous articles, dealing with such German authors as Franz Kafka, Thomas Mann and Hermann Hesse. He has also edited two cultural-historical books about Sanktmartin, a typical German community in Roumania, and has published a book-length study of that community's dialect. To these scholarly works, published from 1951 to 2003, Joseph has added three collections of his own poetry and epigrams: *A Trail of Poetic Reflection.* Berkeley, California: Beatitude Press, 2008, 114 pp.; *A Medley of Piquant Poetry and Edgy Epigrams.* Berkeley, California: Beatitude Press, 2010, 126 pp.; and *More Salt and Pepper. Poems and Epigrams.* Berkeley, California: Beatitude Press, 2012, 173 pp. A critical appraisal of America was the latest of Mileck's many books: *America. An Empire in Disarray.* Berkeley, California: Beatitude Press, 2013, 172 pp.